NOT EVEN WRONG

NOT EVEN WRONG

A Father's Journey into
the Lost History of Autism

PAUL COLLINS

BLOOMSBURY

Published by Bloomsbury Publishing, New York and London
Distributed to the trade by Holtzbrinck Publishers

All papers used by Bloomsbury Publishing are natural, recyclable products
made from wood grown in sustainable, well-managed forests.
The manufacturing processes conform to the environmental
regulations of the country of origin.

The Library of Congress has cataloged the hardcover edition as follows:

Collins, Paul, 1969-
Not even wrong : adventures in autism / Paul Collins.—First U.S. edition.
p. cm.
Includes bibliographical references.
ISBN 1-58234-367-5 (hbk.)
1. Autism in children. 2. Autism in children—Patients—Rehabilitation. 3. Caregivers.
I. Title.
RJ506.A9C645 2004
618.92'85882—dc22
2003017574

First published in the United States by Bloomsbury Publishing in 2004
This paperback edition published in 2005

Paperback ISBN 1-58234-478-7
ISBN-13 9781582344782

1 3 5 7 9 10 8 6 4 2

Typeset by Hewer Text Ltd, Edinburgh
Printed in the United States of America
by Quebecor World Fairfield

CONTENTS

For Morgan

PART ONE

THE WILD BOY

CHAPTER 1

A collapsible steamer basket, opened to its full circumference, resembles a giant perforated metal flower—like something the Iron Giant might wear in his lapel. I never gave it any thought before becoming a parent. But a child forces you to retrace the steps of things that you've forgotten you ever learned, like how to turn a doorknob, how to wash your hands, or how to stare so intently at a kitchen implement that it becomes a completely abstract object.

"Da-ya dicky-doe," Morgan reports, and clatters it aside before racing off to the other end of the house. I look at Jennifer, she looks at me: we shrug. He's two going on three, and he has his own language.

Most days Jennifer has the overnight and the early morning Morgan shift. I have the morning and the evening. The afternoons we usually have off. I clomp upstairs to muse over bound Victorian volumes of *Notes and Queries*, peruse the London papers on-line, rearrange my pens, examine my shoelaces. Sometimes, unbelievably, I write. Jennifer goes into a bedroom scattered over with crossword puzzles, slathered paint palettes, and crunched-out tubes of Winsor & Newton acrylic and emerges with a spiral-bound notebook, headed for her favorite writing table at the local bagel shop. During these afternoons—the closest thing we have to a workday—our son is with Marc, an old friend of ours who has basically become his nanny. But today Morgan's spending the afternoon with us instead.

We follow Morgan to our bedroom, where he is paging through a weighty *Merck Manual* that he's pulled off our bookshelf. He is on cardiovascular disorders, in the early part of the book. He grabs my finger like a pointer, jabbing it at words.

"A . . . doctor . . . may . . . suspect . . . uh, endocarditis . . ."

He jams my finger harder into the word, demanding explanation.

"Morgan, that's . . . oh, that's a hard word."

He pushes my finger away, done with me, and returns to turning pages. He hasn't made it past lymphatic disorders in the manual, which is probably just as well, because the later bits on occupational lung diseases really aren't good reading for children.

"Hey, Morgan," Jennifer says. "Hey, Morgan."

He turns the page.

"Hey, Morgan. We're going to ride in a taxi today. A yellow taxi. All of us. In a yellow taxi."

"Naya," he repeats. This is his word for yellow. "Naya taxi."

"That's right. You're going to ride in a yellow taxi! With Mommy! And Daddy!"

He doesn't look up from the pages, but he has the faintest hint of a smile in his face, undetectable to anyone else.

"Morgan . . ." I sing. "*Mooo-rgan . . .*"

He turns the page, looking even more intent, ignoring me.

"Morr-gan. I know you. I know *you*. I know you're listening."

No.

"Mor-gan. *Morrr* . . . gotcha gotcha gotcha!"

I pounce on him, and he collapses against me in hysterical giggling. It's been the best joke for as long as he can remember.

"Careful, honey bunny." He's tugging at the coiled black wire to the doctor's ear-probe light hanging on the wall. "Gentle. We can't break that."

We can, of course, and probably will.

"Gentle. *Gentle.*"

I root through the supply of toys in Jennifer's messenger bag, the multitudes of card decks, writing materials, and books to keep Morgan occupied while we wait in the doctor's office. Out comes a thin blue hardcover book.

"*Cat!*" Morgan says firmly. "*Hat!*"

And then he immediately turns his attention back to the coil. The door opens; Jennifer and I both look up.

"Hi. I'm Dr. Whalen."

"I'm Jennifer." My wife shakes her hand.

"I'm Paul. And this is Morgan."

"Hello. Hi, Morgan."

Morgan is still busy inspecting the coil, thrumming it back and forth.

"So . . ." The doctor looks at him quizzically over her clipboard. "Three-year checkup?"

"We're a little early for that, actually," Jennifer admits.

"We just moved here," I explain. "It's been a little while since his last checkup, so we just figured . . ."

I trail off. There's not much else to say, since there's nothing actually wrong with him.

"Okay," says the doctor. She gives us the standard questions: are his vaccinations up-to-date, has he been ill lately, and so forth, all while examining his muscular little body. Morgan ignores her. He's studying the buttons on my shirt. She does the usual prodding and poking, and Morgan swats away the lighted ear probe, as any sensible child would.

"How's his hearing?" she asks.

"He can hear me unwrap a Popsicle from across the house."

"Mmm-hmm."

She sets down her clipboard. "Have you had Morgan tested for developmental delays?"

Jennifer and I stare at her blankly.

"What?"

"Your child hasn't said a word in the last five minutes. And"—she retraces her steps through the room—"he didn't look up when I entered, or when I said his name. Or when I shook a toy."

She rattles a rather unimpressive trinket.

"He's a very secure child," I explain. "He doesn't care about you. No offense."

"Morgan," says the doctor, "would you like a sticker?"

She holds up a grim little decal of a teddy bear for several seconds before giving up.

"He didn't even look," she says.

I didn't even look.

"He's like that," Jennifer says. "If he's focused on something, it doesn't matter what you have, and it doesn't matter who comes into a room. He interacts, but only when he feels like it."

"It's not a typical response for his age," the doctor insists. "And he doesn't use language with you, either."

"He does . . . well, what I mean is, he's fascinated by language. He learned his alphabet when he was one."

"Really?"

"Yeah. He reads words now, sentences."

Jennifer pulls out the Magna Doodle, a sort of writable Etch A Sketch that Morgan makes us take everywhere.

"Look," Jennifer says, as much to the doctor as to Morgan. She draws a bunch of rounded fruit and stem and then writes "G R A P E S" underneath.

"*Gwayps!*" Morgan yells.

Then Jennifer writes "D I A M O N D." Before she's even drawn the picture:

"*Di-ya-mond!*"

I turn to the doctor. "He also counts up to twenty."

"That's quite unusual for a two-year-old."

Morgan insistently pulls Jennifer's hand back to the slate. She jots down numbers this time.

"And he counts down," Jennifer adds in a hopeful voice, and I nod enthusiastically, desperately looking for some sign of approval in the doctor's face.

There is none.

"He has a preference for written words over speaking?"

"Yes. I mean, he can talk. He just chooses not to. He doesn't ask for things that way. We try to prompt him, but he won't do it. But he'll repeat songs, things he reads in books."

"So he's not using it to interact."

"Well . . ."

"Two plus fwee . . . *equals* . . . five!" Morgan announces triumphantly.

"That's right!" I stroke his hair and then turn back to the doctor. "He can start up and operate a computer, too."

"But he won't respond to commands?"

He does *arithmetic*. He *reads*.

"Does Morgan resp—"

"No, no. Not as such, no."

"Hmm."

And then she writes something down.

"He understands *us*," Jennifer says. "We understand *him*."

"But he does not socialize or verbalize."

"He plays with us," I explain. "He's a happy kid. He's smart."

The doctor sets down her pen.

"I think," she says, "you may want to consider testing for developmental delays. There may be a cognitive disability."

I can feel myself getting a headache. I turn to look at my son, who is placidly ignoring the whole conversation. He is back to pulling languidly at the ear probe's coiled black cord:

Thwack. Thwack. Thwack.

Morgan's nodded off by the time we get home, and he's still strapped into his toddler car seat when I carry him into the living room. Jennifer and I slump onto the couch and watch him sleep. He looks perfectly content, and yet . . . How can it be that we left our house an hour ago with a healthy toddler, and returned with a disabled one?

"So . . ." I sigh. "Now what?"

"I don't know."

Everything looks different all of a sudden: the way he's sleeping, is that abnormal? The funny sound he makes when he's happy? The fact that we can't get him to say his name but that he likes to repeat things back to us? And yet . . . dammit, there is *nothing wrong with him*. We would have noticed. He . . . *we*—we were doing just fine until today.

"This is ridiculous." I look over the information sheet the doctor gave us for getting him evaluated and toss it aside. "He's fine. He's just different from what they're used to."

Morgan nuzzles against the side of his seat, smacks his lips, and falls blissfully back to sleep.

"I know." There is a long pause. "But we should make an appointment."

"I guess."

It just doesn't make any sense at all. *Nothing has really happened.* He is the same boy that he has always been: we are the same parents that we have always been.

"What if . . ."

Her question hangs in the air.

"They find something?"

She nods.

"They won't."

"But if they do?"

He was in for a checkup, that's all. And . . . and . . . how can this even be happening? Jennifer watches me thinking and rubs my shoulder.

"I'll take him for a while," she says. "You haven't had any time to yourself today."

"I guess."

"We'll be okay," she tells me.

So I climb the creaking steps up to the garret, dodging gaps in the boards and old nails that need setting: I'm the only one who ever goes up here, and fixing it is an ongoing project. I never really finished unpacking from the move, either, and on top of the U-Haul boxes in my office are notes in little piles; old Georgian volumes teeter precariously on the desk, and reams of library photocopies are piled up in snowdrifts everywhere. "Peter," say the Post-its notes hastily stuck to them. In another pile are book drafts about Peter; most of the paragraphs are raggedly scratched out. I can't get it right. There is something missing in them, and I still can't figure out what.

I stop and stare out my window. What if there *is* something wrong?

I turn back to my notes and leaf through them. I first saw Peter last year, when we were living in Wales. I was idly paging through a crumbling leather-bound book I'd found, titled *Eccentric and Remarkable Characters*, and there he was in an engraving: "Peter the Wild Boy." He was looking off into space, or at least off into the margins. I'd never heard of him before. Almost no one has, for no biography has ever been written on Peter. But once, everyone knew of the wild boy and his fantastically strange life—that of the nearly mute feral child who capered through the royal court at Kensington Palace, met Swift and Defoe; who haunted the births of Romanticism, zoology, and even the theory of evolution.

Peter followed me. I moved a couple of times, watched my toddler grow, and wrote some books, but I couldn't quite get him out of my head, and I wasn't sure why. For there was almost nothing to be said about Peter himself. He was a silent enigma; the more I read about him, the more I learned about everybody around him. He was a mirror held up to the great men of his time, reflecting their thoughts and dreams and revealing none of his own. All who gazed at Peter's averted eyes discovered something about themselves instead—and about what it means to be human. It never occurred to me, back then, that I'd become one of those people.

The earliest reports came from boatmen plying the Weser, who'd seen a creature emerging from the Black Forest and lurking on the riverbank. Pitying the ragged animal, the men would toss it scraps of food. But when the town burghers of Hamelin ventured into the forest in July 1725, they scarcely could have been prepared for the sight that confronted them as they approached a remote clearing. For there, unaware of their presence, was that rarest of wild animals: a human.

He appeared to be a boy of about twelve—naked and dirty, his hair long and matted, but unmistakably a boy. The burghers watched him from a distance as he hid in the shelter of a tree hollow, foraging for acorns and grass and pulling up what edible plants he could find. The boy looked up: he fled on all fours, tearing through the field and clambering up a tree. He was climbing like a squirrel, witnesses said. The burghers tracked him silently and surrounded the tree to force him down.

That is one story, at least. There is another, of a local farmer named Meyer Jurgen. Some say that it was Meyer who found him, and not out in the forest. He discovered the boy in a pasture on his farm, sucking greedily from the teat of a cow. The frightened child was torn between running and drinking when he saw the farmer approach; but Meyer, who was used to taming all sorts of animals, coaxed the famished boy indoors with a handful of apples.

Both stories could be true. The boy was impossible to tame and may have already escaped from Meyer when the burghers found him. So in November 1725, the burghers of Hamelin placed their young charge under the watchful eye of a prison warden and imprisoned the boy for safekeeping in a jail in the nearby town of Zell. He was an inmate with neither a crime nor a name; naked and mute, he bore no clue to his origin or identity. A name of convenience was fixed upon the wild, unspeaking creature: Peter.

Once their young inmate had been washed and clothed, Peter's captors were able to see the resemblance between him and other boys in the town. His features were like those of anyone else from the region, his wild mass of hair notwithstanding; save for a bit of webbing between two of his fingers, his body bore no obvious signs of defects that might have caused him to be abandoned. Moreover, he was not exactly mute: he could indeed make sounds, but nothing resembling human speech. He seemed deaf and yet was not quite that, either; for while neither the calling of his name nor the blast of a firearm produced so much as a flinch in the boy, the cracking of a walnut several rooms away could bring him running in eager anticipation. Indeed, as shy as he was, he seemed fairly happy with himself and friendly enough whenever he did take notice of the people around him.

In other regards, the wild boy seemed more animal than human. He would not eat any of the cooked food placed before him, preferring instead his simple wild diet of roots and nuts. Clothes placed on his body were quickly torn off in annoyance, and he would not sleep in a bed when it was made for him. Jailers looking in on Peter would find him curled up on the floor in a corner, slumbering lightly and facing the door in a perpetually alert position.

The only clue to his origins when the burghers found him was the tattered remains of an old shirt collar still around his neck, though whether it was all that remained of the clothes his family or perhaps Meyer Jurgen had once clad him in, no one could be sure. Idle gossip and speculation took the place of any real facts; some thought he might be the unwanted offspring of a local maiden and one of the criminals locked up at the Zell jail; others opined that he was an orphaned idiot. Such secrets will seep out in a small village, yet there was no word of who the miscreant parents might be. Nor was it clear that Peter was an idiot child, for he was alert and inquisitive— happy, even. Yet he was indefinably *different*. But who was to say what years in the wilderness might have wrought upon even the most normal child?

Days passed, and no parent or relative stepped forward to claim their wild boy. Peter was alone in the world—in his very own world, in fact, since he would not talk or even meet anyone's gaze. His one great pleasure remained being taken outside to roam in the fields.

I am being shaken lightly.

"They're here. They're here. They're early."

"Mmm?"

It is eight-thirty, an hour and a half before my shift starts; I was up till three A.M. writing.

"They're outside," Jennifer insists. "I need you to hold Morgan while I clear a space for them."

I rub my eyes, pull on my pants, and stagger out into the living room. It is unnaturally cold in our new house, a creaking old Victorian; the piano movers have our front door open to lay down mats and pads, preparing to move in the century-old bruiser of an upright piano that we inherited from Jen's grandmother. It's been in storage at a friend's house for over a year, while we moved from San Francisco to rural Wales and then finally back to settle here in Oregon.

Morgan is still in his pajamas at the other end of the room, paying no attention to the movers. He is standing on a low chair propped against a table, busily tapping away at his iMac.

"Morgan, wait till you see this. Our *piano*. We're getting our piano back."

He does not look up but acknowledges my presence by leaning into me. I give his blond hair a little tousle and kiss his head; he smiles a little and leans some more, until all his weight is slumped against me. But he does not look up; he keeps clicking away at his arithmetic program.

"Four," he says. "Fi-yive."

A trio of burly movers come through the door and nod good morning.

"Smart kid," one says.

"Yeah."

"You want it by this wall?" another mover asks Jennifer.

She is moving a couple of her large canvases out of the way.

"Sure, that's perfect."

The house's scarred old floorboards are groaning: The piano rumbles in through the front door, propped up on a giant handcart, enormously heavy and suspended and perilous.

Morgan bolts from his chair for it: I snatch him up, wriggling.

"Wait, Morgan. *Wait*. It's dangerous now, they're still moving it."

The men slowly set the piano down: as its treble end touches ground with a little thud, a ghostly chord sighs out of it. I let Morgan down and he scrambles over to the piano. *Plink plink bruuum*: his hands dash madly up and down the keyboard, he stretches his arms out at full length to span three octaves and batters his hands against the white keys until a C-major roar fills the room.

He stops to leap up and down. "Yay! Yayy! *Yayyyyyy!*"

Then he pumps in a bunch of breath, hyperventilating, rattles his head, and batters away at the keyboard for another five minutes solid while Jennifer writes a check to the moving guy, who is watching in unabashed fascination at the performance.

"Yes no ABCDEFG Twinkle Twinkle!" Morgan hollers as his fists pound out time on the keys.

Then he stops for a moment and cranes his head all the way back, with a blissed-out smile at the ceiling: The note resonates and decays for a second.

"*Aaaaaaah-yee!*" he begins again.

The movers pick up the floor pads and leave, the roar following them out the door. Jennifer and I look at each other, then at our child assaulting the piano.

"So," she yells over the cacophony, "still going back to bed?"

I can hear the piano rumbling up into the floorboards as my finger traces over the old map. "Hanover," reads the spidery font.

There were, in the year of 1725, two great local personages in the province. The first was Peter, a tanned wild child that no German could begin to make sense of. The second was the elector of Hanover—a pale little nobleman whom none of his subjects could make any sense of, either. In 1714 the elector had been saddled with a job that no sensible Hanoverian could possibly want: he'd become George I, bearer of the British crown. George was not the worst king Britain ever had, but he was its least willing. After ten years on the throne, the reluctant monarch had still not bothered to learn the language of the rain-soaked island that he inherited; when he tired of killing time with scientific curiosities or his brace of mistresses, he would eagerly flee the damp confines of London for long vacations in his beloved homeland. And so it was that a king, one evening in November 1725, had dinner in Hanover with its other most famous native son—a speechless boy without a friend in the world.

Peter was ushered by his keepers into the royal dining room, where the king waited with the evening meal. Peter may have been the only person in the room who was not the least bit mindful of His Majesty. Instead, the boy happily commenced with his usual favorite activities when presented with a roomful of strangers: clambering over people as if they were climbing walls, with a carefree obliviousness to their discomfort as he trod merrily on laps and shoulders.

King George watched the boy, fascinated. A napkin was pinned to Peter, and the king urged him to try each of the dishes set before them. The king's dinner was surely the most sumptuous spread of food the poor creature had ever seen. But Peter was not much interested in fine cuisine: he pushed aside bread and savories, eating only the nuts and beans that he could identify from the forest. He saved his greatest gusto for asparagus and especially raw onions, which he ate like apples, and after finishing them, he expressed his approval by beating his chest. The whole spectacle was so uncouth that the boy had to be led away to protect the decorum of the king's presence. But George was not offended—indeed, one witness noted, "His Majesty has ordered that he has such provisions as [Peter] likes best, and that he may have such instruction as may best befit him for human society."

Peter proved to be singularly unimpressed with the prospect of fitting into human society. Before long he was discovered missing and tracked back down to the Black Forest, where he was found hiding again in his favorite tree. He'd had enough of civilization and would not climb down from his tree—whereupon the town worthies felled it with hatchets. As Peter was led away, he could not know that he would never see his Black Forest home again. The world had other plans for him.

"So," Autumn tells us, "we're going to do this evaluation by setting up some activities for him to do, and it's sort of timed."

Morgan is sitting on a carpet at the child development center, running a toy pickup truck back and forth in an arc across the floor. The room is full of grown-ups—me, Jennifer, and a clutch of

women bearing business cards that all read PORTLAND EARLY IN-
TERVENTION PROGRAM—and our son could not care less. He is
holding up the pickup truck and spinning its wheels one by one, then
in pairs, then all at once, carefully observing how they slow
themselves to a halt by friction or by his slapping a hand against
their treads.

Autumn, the newly minted college grad of the group, goes over to
a video camera at the corner of the room, adjusts its tripod angle
downward, and then slips a tape into a boom box. The specialists sit
at a table in one corner, observing our son. Autumn turns on the tape
and then drops down on her haunches to Morgan's height.

"Okay! Morgan, we're going to have fun."

He looks up momentarily from his truck and then goes back to
spinning the wheels.

"Ready," the disembodied voice warbles from the boom box. *Beep.*

"Okay!" Autumn says. "Morgan, let's play with blocks."

She pulls out a set of wooden blocks and takes one out.

"Can you take out a wooden block?"

He looks at the bag in a desultory way.

"I take a block out," she says. "Can you take one out?"

Morgan turns around to look at the video camera and boom box
instead.

"Ready," it says again. *Beep.*

Jennifer and I look at each other. What are they getting at here?

"Morgan . . . Morgan," Autumn repeats. "Where is the red
block? Where is the red—"

He mashes his finger down on the red block.

"Good! Where is the yellow block?"

He gets that one, too. He keeps wanting to look back at the
camera instead, but at least he's getting the questions right now.

Jennifer reaches over and squeezes my hand, and I feel a burden lifting off me. We desperately want to intervene and cheer him on, but we both have to keep quiet.

"Where is the bl—"

"Ready," it says.

Morgan spins around to face the boom box.

"*Set!*" he yells back delightedly. "*Go!*"

Laughter ripples through the room.

Beep.

"Morgan . . ." Autumn smiles. "Can you look at the doggie here? The doggie? . . . Morgan?"

The "Ready" keeps coming, and each time, Morgan turns around to yell, "Set! Go!" back at the boom box. This, he has decided, is the point of the game. He is barely paying attention to Autumn and her bag of toys.

"Morgan, can you clap your hands? Like this? . . . Morgan? . . . Morgan, look at me. Clap. Clap your—"

"Ready."

"Set!" he yells. "Go!"

Beep.

He turns to Autumn but notices her case file folder and reaches into it.

"No, Morgan," she says cheerily as he rearranges paperwork. "Over here . . . Morgan?"

Autumn waits until he is looking back at her, and then she deliberately pulls her lips into a sad-face frown.

"*Ohhh,*" she sobs woefully, waiting for his sympathy. "Ohhh! Boo-hoo!"

He watches her a moment but doesn't react. Then he gets up and walks away.

"Ready."

"Set! Go!"

He charges at the big expensive video camera and grabs the tripod, and all of us—a roomful of half a dozen adults—are frozen for a moment.

Beep.

"Whoa!" I swoop in. "Morgan, no no no. Leave the camera alone."

"Cam-wa."

"That's right, honey. Let's go back and see Autumn."

But he pulls against me. He doesn't want Autumn or her toys or her funny faces. He wants to inspect the tripod.

"Morgan—"

"Ready."

"Set! Go!"

I keep waiting for them to end the test, because it's all falling apart now, but they don't. It just keeps going, and the timed beeps won't stop, and the camera doesn't stop rolling, and he misses out on more and more of the evaluation prompts. And the specialists take more and more notes.

CHAPTER 2

The summons came in March of 1726: Bring him to London.

Peter made the long voyage over land and then by sea, an unimaginable journey for one who just a few months before had scarcely seen anything beyond his own grove of trees. Drawing near to London, he had a privilege afforded to few of even the most respectable citizens of his home village: the sight of the largest and mightiest city in Europe. Onward his party continued into the city, into its very heart and to the gates of St. James's Palace. This palace was not really all that palatial, having originally served as a home "for the use of leprous women," but over the years it had been converted into a comfortable royal residence, and it was where George preferred to spend his winter months in London.

Peter had, by this time, been encouraged into walking more or less upright rather than on all fours, as had been his wont when first discovered. Dressed to meet royalty, he and his party were escorted through the outer piazza by the king's armed yeomen, up a grand staircase, through a guardroom, and then past a state room where ambassadors were received. But Peter was only an ambassador for the raw and wild state of Humanity itself, so from there he was led down to the Great Drawing-Room, which was the true center of court life. Several days a week, nobility and ministers flocked there to politely angle for the attention of the royal family. It was also the best place in court to size up newcomers, for the Great Drawing-Room was used to welcome visiting royalty, nobility, or foreign curiosities. The court could hardly have imagined anything, though, like the wordless boy brought before them.

On April 5, the London newspaper *Wye's Letter* reported on Peter's reception at the court:

[Peter] was carried last Friday into the presence of his Majesty, and many of the nobility. He is supposed to be about thirteen years old, and scarce seems to have any idea of things; however, 'tis observed that he took most notice of his Majesty, and of the Princess giving him her glove, which he tried to put on his own hand, and seemed much pleased, as also with a gold watch, which was held to strike at his ear. They put on him blue clothes; but he seemed uneasy to be obliged to wear any . . . We hear he is committed to the care of Dr. Arbuthnot, in order to try if he can be brought to the use of speech, and made a sociable creature.

Some courtiers may have got a little more entertainment than they bargained for that night, given Peter's fondness for turning out people's pockets to look for treats. Afterward there were attempts "to warn all Ladies and Gentlemen who intend to Visit this Wild Man, not to carry any Thing in their Pockets that is indecent, to prevent Accidents for the future."

Civilizing such a boy would require a great talent, so the king put him into the capable hands of Dr. Arbuthnot, who was highly esteemed as a court physician. It was a mark of the man's talents to have a court job title: the composer then serving the court, for example, was none other than Georg Handel. Peter was to live at

Arbuthnot's house in the city, and it is hard to imagine a better time or place for an impressionable boy to have been dropped into the middle of London society. Arbuthnot's scientific colleagues at the Royal Society included Edmond Halley and the elderly Isaac Newton. Arbuthnot was also esteemed as one of the great literary wits of London and had a "Scribbler's Club" with his close friends Jonathan Swift and Alexander Pope. Both had frequent occasion to stop by the good doctor's home. Amid all this, the comings and goings of London life—and particularly Peter's dramatic arrival—were under the watchful eye of Daniel Defoe and the essayists Addison and Steele. The simple boy from the Black Forest had landed squarely in what was, for all purposes, the center of his era's intellectual universe.

Writing to his friend Thomas Tickell on April 16, Jonathan Swift marveled: "This night I saw the wild boy, whose arrival here hath been the subject of half our talk this fortnight. He is in the keeping of Dr. Arbuthnot, but the King and Court were so entertained with him, that the Princess could [not] get him till now." The king's daughter-in-law, Princess Caroline, had such a great fondness for the unaffected and silent boy from the outset—it was her watch that had been held up to his ear, and he was utterly fascinated by the bejeweled black velvet dress she wore—that she pleaded with the king to let her keep Peter among her own coterie. Indeed, the prospect of meeting a wild boy seemed to arouse a peculiar amount of interest among other ladies of the court, as Swift tartly observed:

His being so young was Occasion of the great Disappointment of the Ladies, who came to the Drawing Room in full Expectation of some Attempt upon their Chastity: So far is true, that he endeavoured to kiss the young Lady W——le, who for that reason is become the

Envy of the Circle; this being a Declaration of Nature, in favour of her superior Beauty.

Charming as such pronouncements by nature to Prime Minister Walpole's wife were, the king had resolved that his young charge should at length become civilized. The first step toward civilization was already well-known from the empire's years of experience in colonizing foreign lands. On July 5, in Dr. Arbuthnot's garden, Peter the Wild Boy was baptized.

"Okay!" I yell. "It's ready."

I put my hand under the shower head one more time to make sure the water's the right temperature. We've tried everything—playing in the bathtub, reading books about taking a bath, taking baths first ourselves to show there's nothing to be afraid of, and on and on. Nothing works. He hates it, he fears it, and it's now a two-person shower job. We just try to get him in and out as fast as possible.

The bathroom door opens and Jennifer carries him in. He is curled up against her body, clinging tightly to her shirt.

"Hey, Morgan! We're going to get all clean."

"Let go, honey," she says to him. "C'mon. Let go of Mommy's shirt. Let go let go let go."

He whimpers and looks up fearfully.

"It's okay, it's okay. You'll get all clean now. It'll be really fast."

"It's okay. Honey, it's okay."

We make the handoff, and now he fastens to me in the shower. The water runs over his naked body, and he is whimpering louder, burying his head into my shoulder.

"Morgan, it's okay." I stroke his head, guiding water over his hair. "We're just getting your hair wet now. It's okay."

Jennifer works a squirt of baby shampoo in while singing to him. "Sham-poo, sham-poo, sham-poo . . ." The suds run over his face.

"*Aaayyy!*" he shrieks, and flails. He gets a foothold against one side of the shower and kicks hard against it; we stagger toward Jennifer, who stands outside the shower, and she pushes our listing mass back in.

"Morgan, shh-shh-sh-sh, calm down."

"It's okay, honey, we're rinsing off, it's okay . . ."

He sobs, clutching me while pushing away at me all at once, and I keep on holding to his slippery shape because it is impossible and because there is no other way.

Five minutes later, he is bouncing wildly on our bed like it's a trampoline, shaking his wet hair and singing along with Big Bird on the TV.

— G! —

— H! —

— I! —

— J! —

— K! —

— L! —

He has already forgotten the shower.

We've never had a state employee of any kind over, so we're scrubbing ourselves and our home as if we'll be led away in leg irons if she sees the dust under the sofas.

"So when is . . ." I stop the motion of the broom for a moment. "I can't remember her name . . ."

Jennifer rinses off another dish. "Mindy."

"When is she getting here again?"

Jennifer looks up at the clock. "Now."

"Ah." I sweep and dustpan faster. "That's what I thought."

"*Giddyap! Wahoo!*" Morgan yells from the backyard. He is piggybacking and bouncing around on Marc's shoulders, the better to get him to canter faster. "*Waaa-hooo!*" Marc sees me through the window, looks up at Morgan, and shrugs with besieged amusement.

Jennifer gets the last of the dishes away and pushes a jumbled stack of her stretcher bars and canvases into a closet; I grab her grandmother's tarnished old silver teapot out of the cabinet, cram it with flowers, and fuss with arranging it in the living room. Water slops onto the table. The doorbell rings, and I stuff stray petals into my pocket and wipe up the water with my sleeve.

"Can you get the door, honey?" Jennifer yells.

"Um . . ."

"*Pecos Bill!*"

"I'll get it."

Mindy comes through the front door and Morgan through the back simultaneously, and I am in the middle of the room, unready.

"Hi, I'm Mindy." She shakes Jennifer's hand and then mine. I can feel my sleeve is soggy. "We met last week at the evaluation."

"I remember." I smile. "Hi."

Morgan cannonballs past us. "*Yee-hah!*"

"There he is!" she chirps, and leans down. "Hi, Morgan! Hello!"

He gallops a circuit around the room, ignoring her.

"He was outside playing horsie with Uncle Marc," Jennifer explains.

"That's the baby-sitter?"

"*Yee-hah!*"

"Yes," I say, and nod, though baby-sitter isn't really the word for it. Marc's become the Uncle Zonker to my Doonesbury, an off-kilter painter whose palette box now also contains baby wipes and juice boxes.

"And Morgan communicates well with his baby-sitter?"

"Oh, Marc's great with him. He's known him since he was born."

Which is almost true. Marc took the day off from his job at an art supply store and visited the hospital the morning labor was induced. Morgan didn't want to come out. It went on and on, dragging into the middle of the night, and we finally, mercifully, told Marc he was a good friend and to go home and get some sleep. But the labor was going badly—the fetal distress monitor was revving up, the doctor and I watched Morgan trying to emerge and failing, and Jennifer didn't know, and I thought I could see my son dying before my eyes, dying before he was even born, and I couldn't tell her because she needed to keep pushing . . . well, she didn't need to, actually, because by one A.M. we were in the operating room for a C-section.

When morning broke, and Marc visited again, Jennifer and Morgan were alive and well and sleeping lightly. I was curled up in a hospital chair. When I looked up, I could see sky and trees through a window. I could hear birds singing.

Peter longed above all else for the sun and the open air. There were fine gardens to roam in around St. James; later in the year, when court life shifted over to Kensington Palace, Peter loved to be taken out to lope about the capacious park greens and promenades surrounding the palace. Here the wild boy was exposed to the public at large—perhaps a little too exposed, as the park was a favored cruising area of women for hire. But the boy was oblivious to women's attentions; he was oblivious, in fact, to nearly everything outside of himself. And he certainly did not care what impression he made as he was led about the palace greens.

His effect on others in the park was genuinely unsettling. It was common enough for fashionable ladies at the time to keep monkeys and similar exotica; it was altogether another thing to see a feral child being led about. One traveling French nobleman, Cesar de Saussure, wrote to his family back home:

> I was much struck with his appearance, and remarked that his clothes seemed to hinder his movements. He couldn't bear his hat on his head, but kept throwing it down in the ground. His eyes were haggard, and did not rest on any object, and he looked so wild and extraordinary I cannot describe the impression he made. He frightened me.

Although he may have looked it, Peter was scarcely a danger to other people, whose presence he seldom deigned to notice anyway. But his keepers did have to keep a close watch over him. The first time he had been taken out for a walk, in St. James's Park, Peter was so overjoyed to be reunited with the woodland again that he broke free and clambered up the highest tree—and, once again, refused to come down.

All this was watched with increasing fascination by London's literati. Peter had been a subject of conversation in the papers even weeks before his arrival; now he was everywhere. A London druggist quickly published a pamphlet describing the boy and pondering his origins, proposing that the boy survived winter in the wilderness thanks to the kindness of a bear. "A Bear is the longest suckling and rearing its cubs of any Creature," he theorized, ". . . so that it might with no natural Difficulty attend this infant." But the druggist's pamphlet was less interested in Peter than in selling a wondrous lotion for "the Cure of the *Secret Disease* . . .

accompanied with Smarting of the Urine," as well as a special "Chymical" remedy whose discretion was assured: "The Word ITCH is not mentioned on the Paper that is Pasted on the Bottle."

Still, the druggist had correctly intuited what would keep many minds occupied for the next few months. The *Edinburgh Evening Courant* mused over "a youth who is one of the greatest curiosities that has appeared in the world since the time of Adam . . . how he supported himself in uncomfortable solitude, is at present what takes up the conversation of the learned." Daniel Defoe weighed in with his own pamphlet on Peter, *Mere Nature Delineated*, for the *Robinson Crusoe* author was no stranger to the topic of how a castaway might fend for himself in the wilderness. Others chose to play up the wild boy for satire: a mocking pamphlet titled *The Most Wonderful Wonder That Ever Appeared to the Wonder of the English Nation* soon appeared, followed inevitably by a countersatire titled *The Most Blunderful Blunder*. The first is so thick with veiled references to courtiers that, at the end, the author promises to reveal the real names "if any one will enter into a Bond of £900,000,000 to indemnify the Author." Then again, this also comes after a promise that the author's next work will be titled *A Dissertation upon Pissing*.

Jonathan Swift used his personal knowledge of the boy to knock out his own anonymous satire, *It Cannot Rain but It Pours*. Amid his jokes about how "the new sect of Herb-eaters intend to follow him into the Fields," he also pondered how "he expresseth his Joy most commonly by Neighing . . . a more noble Expression of that Passion than Laughing." Perhaps, Swift mused, "he will serve in Time as an Interpreter between us and other Animals." Indeed, the author was so taken with the enigma of wild humanity presented by Peter that he immediately returned to the subject, this time portraying intelligent neighing horses and feral human beings in a satirical tale that he sent anonymously to a publisher later that year. Swift named his human animals Yahoos—and the tale, *Gulliver's Travels*.

Curiously, the one London writer who remained silent through the whole affair was Dr. Arbuthnot himself. Perhaps this should not be surprising, given that he had his hands full raising a feral child. At first, even getting him to dress was a challenge. Peter could not abide wearing a hat, or almost any other kind of garment, though he had a child's keen fascination with finery—he loved soft cloth and anything that sparkled. It was soon discovered that, fittingly enough, the wild boy of the forest would willingly wear a suit of green cloth. He even became enthusiastically proud of it and wore it constantly.

More important, Arbuthnot made some progress in getting the boy to speak—though Peter does not seem to have enjoyed his lessons. It did not help that teaching methods of the time dictated whipping the occasional leather strap across Peter's legs, "to keep him in awe." But with enough prompting, Peter could be made to repeat letters, his name, and some monosyllabic words. Curiously, he did not use this language the way one might expect—that is, to express his needs or wants. Words had to be pried out of him, and he ignored further attempts to continue into actual conversation. He was a genuinely friendly and imitative boy with remarkably good hearing; he simply did not want to talk.

"Morgan? . . . Morgan?" the specialist asks. "What's your favorite toy?"

He rides off into his bedroom. "Elmo's an old cowhand," we hear him say from inside, to no one, like an afterthought.

Mindy turns to us.

"Well, I'd just like to observe Morgan a bit in his home

environment"—she gestures around—"and see how he interacts with you. And then we'll . . . What lovely old books!"

She nods at our piano; on top is a teetering pile of ancient Victorian tomes that look like they belong in Roderick Usher's library. A volume titled *Desultoria: Recovered MSS of an Eccentric* sits squarely in the middle.

"Yeah, we're overrun with the stuff." I eye the piano and its load of books. "I expect it'll send us crashing through into the basement by next year."

Morgan walks back in, quietly shuffling a deck of arithmetic cards. He loves arranging and rearranging cards. We are constantly having to buy decks for him; every time we go into a supermarket or drugstore, he'll just grab them off the shelf, tear them open, and they're ours.

"Seven," he announces flatly after examining one. He grabs my hand and pulls me over to an old comfy chair and thrusts my hand into the cushion.

"You want me to sit down with you?"

I sit down and he nestles up into my lap, examining more cards.

"Morgan," Mindy asks him, "what are you looking at? What are those?"

"Four."

"What is that?" she presses. "Is that a card?"

"Four," he whispers.

I look down at the card.

3 + 1

I look up, but they have moved on to Morgan's room, where Jennifer is showing Mindy around. I stroke Morgan's hair.

"You're a very smart boy," I whisper in his ear.

I like to imagine that someday the two of us will play practical jokes on people's cognition, by passing them bad math the way you give someone spiked punch at a party:

$$\text{Let } x = y$$
$$\text{Then } x^2 = xy$$
$$\text{therefore, } x^2 - y^2 = xy - y^2$$
$$\text{therefore, } (x + y) (x - y) = y (x - y)$$
$$\text{therefore, } x + y = y$$
$$\text{therefore, } 2y = y$$
$$\textit{therefore:}$$
$$2 = 1$$

"Fouuurr," he repeats, and files away his card.

Morgan is lying on his bedroom rug, his body in a right angle with legs stuck straight up in the air, and he is staring at a sheet of stickers with pictures of musical instruments. We sit watching from his bed.

"Do you like music, Morgan?"

"Music."

He pulls a sticker off the sheet.

"Tuba," he adds dreamily.

"That's right!" Mindy gushes. "That's a tuba. Do you like the tuba? A tuba goes *boom boom. Boom.*"

Jennifer and I look at each other as Morgan darts out of the room and Mindy follows. *Boom?* I mouth wordlessly. Jennifer shrugs and rolls her eyes. It takes a few minutes until it dawns on me: oh, right. Mindy's testing him. When we emerge into the living room, Morgan is bouncing around impatiently, waiting for his computer to boot up.

"Isosceles triangle!" Morgan streaks past us. "Rhombus!"

He's been going through a geometric phase. He leaps effortlessly onto a couch, scrambles onto its arm, and jumps down onto the cushion, rebounds off onto the floor, and ricochets onto a rocking chair. This he stands on while expertly balancing himself and wobbling the chair under his feet.

"We've thought of covering the house in gym mats," I admit.

"Does he often do this, climbing onto furniture? Like that?"

"Um, well, not like . . . I mean, not specifically. He'll climb anything. He just likes climbing and jumping."

"*Whoa!*" Morgan whoops. He hauls out the bench from under the piano and climbs it, too. The velvet upholstery has long been torn off by his gymnastics; it's now down to the original faded pink Edwardian fabric. Morgan vaults gracefully off the bench: *whump.*

"And so there's been no physical problems? No awkwardness? Clumsiness? Epilepsy?"

"Oh no, no. He's been perfect."

He *is* perfect . . . well, perfect to us. But we felt as though our inevitable parental pride had the outside world's stamp of approval; as a baby in San Francisco, he was cute enough to get scouted out of a crowd by a photographer working for the Gap. Would we come in for a Baby Gap test shoot? We felt simultaneously wary and not a little flattered. There was something unsettling about the idea of modeling our child, even if just for a pajama suit with bunnies all over it—but we needn't have worried. Jennifer took him to their studio, but the shoot just couldn't begin. Morgan would smile when he felt like it and not smile when he was asked to. He wanted to examine the photographer's gear; he couldn't care less about the photographer. He didn't say "cheese"; didn't watch the birdie; didn't notice the toys and rattles the assistants were shaking. The photographer and crew were stumped.

"Sorry," Jennifer had offered to the crew, while being politely shown the door. "He's not a people person."

CHAPTER 3

What does it mean to be *a person*? To be human?

In the eighteenth century it was a very tangible and specific question: tales had been filtering back for years from explorers of other races, of strange lands and customs, and of newly found varieties of apes that bore an unnerving resemblance to humans. There were also lands of one-legged men, countries of men with long tails, and a South American race of men with eyes in their breasts—at least, that's what the sailors were claiming. With the rise of Enlightenment science, arranging and naming this wildly divergent array of earthly creation began in earnest, and determining what was and wasn't human became a serious concern among philosophers.

When Peter the Wild Boy arrived in London, even the most basic categories of biology were still up for grabs; it was hard to know just where one form of life began and another ended. The scholars of the Royal Academy had only recently managed to stamp out the reports of a plant in China whose pods, when ripened, broke open to reveal tiny lambs inside. In England itself, a similar story had persisted with so-called barnacle geese. These extraordinary birds were thought to begin life as barnacles that when cast up on shore would grow into trees that bore a shell-like fruit. John Gerarde, the father of English botany, reported what happened next:

When it is perfectly formed the shell gapeth wide open, and the first thing that appeareth is the aforesaid lace or string; next come the legs of the bird hanging out, and as it groweth greater it openeth the shell by degrees, till at length it has all come forth, and hangeth only by the bill. In short space it cometh to full maturity, and falleth into the sea, where it gathereth feathers, and groweth to a fowl.

Beginning life as a fish, taking root as a tree, and then ending as a fowl: It sounded incredible, but enough credence had been given to the story that it was considered acceptable to eat barnacle geese during Lent, since they were more fish than fowl.

In a slippery world full of strange metamorphoses, who was to say just where the animal realm ended and the human began? The one question about Peter the Wild Boy that had been on everyone's minds after he was discovered was: who was he? But over time, a much more unsettling one took shape.

What was he?

Well, he was most certainly uneducated, and at length it was decided that he needed to be sent to school. As a charge of the royal family, no mere local tutorial would do for Peter; he was to go to Harrow School. Perhaps a feral child's admission at Harrow was not inconsistent with rest of the student body; nonetheless, subsequent alumni have included Lord Byron and Winston Churchill. The wild boy who had been living in the trees just months before was now to receive the finest education in the land. He was packed off to the suburbs of London to live with Mrs. King, a matron who ran a boarding-house for students at the school.

On June 3, 1727, the *British Journal* carried a doleful bit of news:

Epitaph on PETER, the Wild Youth, Occasioned by the Report of his Death

YE Yahoos mourn, for in this Place
Lies dead the Glory of your Race;
One, who from Adam had descent
Yet ne'er did what he might repent;
But liv'd, unblemished, to Fifteen,
And yet (O strange!) a Court had seen! . . .

It was a shockingly quick end for the boy who lived so long in the wilderness, to die instead among the ivied halls of Harrow, scarcely months after being immortalized in *Gulliver's Travels*. Indeed, no one would have been more surprised by this turn of events than Peter himself . . . particularly since he was still alive.

But one week after the greatly exaggerated reports of Peter's death, King George fell gravely ill while on yet another trip back to his beloved home in Hanover. He never did make it back to the Black Forest that he and his young charge had left behind; within days he was dead, and Peter the Wild Boy was left without the only man he had ever called his father. George's actual son, the Prince of Wales, had never got on very well with his father; for years the two had scarcely been on speaking terms. Now the father was gone and the son crowned George II. Not surprisingly, the new king was not keen on keeping his father's tiresome freaks and playthings about. Peter's lessons at Harrow had not shown much progress, but the happily unaware boy was now not particularly welcome at court, either.

Fortunately, Peter did still have one true friend in the world: Caroline, the princess who had now become queen. She quietly arranged for her chambermaid, Alice Titchbourn, to take care of the boy. For Alice's troubles, she would receive a royal pension of £30 each year, a generous sum back then. Caring for a feral child was not easy, and the alien setting didn't help; the boy was in the city, but clearly the city was never going to be in the boy. Mrs. Titchbourn moved her charge to a relative's farm outside London, in the farming village of Berkhamsted. Peter, at long last, was free to roam in the countryside once again.

Peter's days on the farm of James Fenn were happy ones; villagers would find the boy humming and singing with pleasure. Nature was closer here; the ripening sun, the crisp nighttime skies, and the passing of the seasons brought real joy to the wild child. One witness noted: "He appeared remarkably animated by the spring, singing all day; and if it was clear, half the night. He is much pleased by the sight of the moon and stars; he will sometimes stand out in the warmth of the sun, with his face turned up towards it in a strained attitude, and he likes to be out in a starry night, if not cold." Bad weather, though, clearly upset him: long before it arrived, he would begin howling in dismay.

But Peter's greatest love was to sit by the fire in the farmhouse. Fire fascinated him: even on the most sweltering day, he would gleefully haul load after load of firewood into the house until he was made to stop. Then he'd drag over and arrange five or six chairs in front of the fire; then rearrange them; then rearrange them yet again. All the while he would hop back and forth from chair to chair, viewing the fire from this angle, then that one, never growing tired of the game.

When his farm family tired of it, though, they had one ploy that always worked: bread and milk. These had become immovably associated in Peter's mind with bedtime; if presented with them, even in broad daylight, he would obediently go upstairs to his bedroom. It never took much to feed Peter, really: The most remarkable feature of his diet was that he ate little and simply, taking his greatest joy in raw cabbage leaves and onions, and drank enormous quantities of water. The wild boy's body was almost supernaturally powerful on this diet, so much so that local boys dared not tease him. Fortunately for them, he was very slow to anger: but when provoked, he would chase tormentors while making a hair-raising growl, and bite at them. Bullies quickly learned not to repeat the experiment.

Bullying would not have achieved much anyway: you could not *make* him do anything. The simplest requests went unheard. Yet when left alone, Peter would unexpectedly join the Fenns at laboring and do the work of three men. His logic about farm tasks was a little different from that of the other workers, though, as one oft repeated tale of Peter recalled:

> Peter was one day engaged with his master in filling a dung-cart. His master had occasion to go into the house, and left Peter to finish the work. But as Peter must be usefully employed, he saw no reason why he should not be as usefully employed in emptying the cart as he had been in filling it. On his master's return, he found the cart nearly emptied again.

To explain the error to Peter was as useless as asking him to do the task in the first place. He could hear, but he didn't listen. In fact, he could hear very well: he was passionately fond of music and would clap and stamp his feet until ready to drop from exhaustion; long afterward, he could be heard humming tunes over and over until he'd got them right.

The last man in Berkhamsted to be so famed for his mysterious nature was probably Henry Axtel, a rich local who had inexplicably starved himself to death in 1625. But over time Peter became a fixture of Berkhamsted: everyone knew who he was. James Fenn eventually passed away, as did the queen who had sent him there; but Peter remained. James's brother Thomas Fenn, who worked another farm in the village, took over, and life continued much the same as before. Years passed, seasons wheeled by over the head of the figure who stood half the day and night in the yard, singing to the skies, and the strange and innocent creature's title remained the same among the villagers: the wild boy.

Even if he was no longer at court much anymore, Peter did leave his visage behind. Peter's stay at Kensington Palace coincided with that of William Kent. A grand staircase designed by Christopher Wren needed redecoration, and Kent was offered £500 for the job. He cleverly turned the walls and ceiling into a painted galley of eternal courtiers, immortalizing the king's most prominent friends and hangers-on, who all appear to be leaning over a painted railing to gaze down upon the visitors coming up the stairs. Kent's work still survives in the palace today. Among the portraits of elaborately dressed mistresses, noblemen, and pages, there he is: Peter, with his wild uncombed hair and resplendent in his favorite green suit. But he is alone in the crowd—averting his eyes and gazing wordlessly into the silence.

Peter never really had left the mind of the public; his portrait was also painted at least twice in his adulthood, and one hung for years in a popular curiosity gallery on Fleet Street. Scholars also found themselves mulling over his case again and again through the years. The wild boy had been confounding philosophers from the day he first set foot in London; he was a perplexing combination of intelligence and obliviousness. Defoe, writing his pamphlet on Peter in 1726, was at loss for how the boy could think without the use of language. "Words are, to us, the Medium of Thought; we cannot conceive of Things, but by their Names."

Yet on second thought, Defoe wondered whether perhaps his curious state made Peter more fortunate than all the rest of London society:

> I confess, to act as a Man, and to have no Pride, no Ambition, no Avarice, no Rancour or Malice, no ungovern'd Passion, no unbounded Desires, how infinitely more happy is he than Thousands of his more inform'd and better-taught fellow Brutes in human Shape, who are every day raging with Envy . . . Had Nature been beneficent in him, in bestowing something more upon him other ways, and yet kept his Soul lock'd as to these Things, how he had been the happiest of all the Race of Rationals in the World?

Defoe's musing did not strike everyone as an exaggeration. "Man is born free; and everywhere he is in chains," Jean-Jacques Rousseau lamented in *The Social Contract* in 1762—an opening line that reverberated for decades into the Romantic movement. To Rousseau, Peter was the very archetype of the noble savage, representing humanity in its pure state.

By every physiological measure, Peter was clearly a human. Yet the young Swedish scholar Carolus Linnaeus, who virtually invented the field of modern zoology, found Peter a peculiar creature to categorize. Linnaeus had traveled widely and had a critical cast of mind; he'd ventured to the Arctic Circle to study the flora of Lapland and later had to flee Hamburg after unmasking a local "seven-headed hydra" exhibit as a fake. Fresh from these adventures, he published his groundbreaking 1735 work, *Systema Naturae*. The young man's genius lay in methodically sorting each member of the natural world into kingdom, order, species, and genus—an innovation that remains the organizing principle behind zoology. Laying down his foundations for this system, he knew that the famous boy simply could not be ignored, so Linnaeus awarded Peter a classification all his own: *Juvenis hannoveranus*. Peter was, moreover, a new variety of the species altogether: *Homo ferus*, the wild man.

And then he was gone.

It had been twenty-four years since Peter had settled into his adoptive home, so long that scarcely anyone would recall how wild he had once been in his youth—or how prone he'd been to breaking loose. Yet in 1751, something awakened in the forty-year-old wild boy. He was so fond of roaming about that his absence would scarcely have been noticed at first. But then the hours turned to days and the days to weeks. It became clear that Peter, the eternal boy with scarcely a word in his mouth or a penny in his pockets, had run away.

Much later, a scruffy man was picked up for questioning in Norwich. He could not give any account of himself or what he was doing in town. This, to the authorities, was clear evidence that the fellow was a spy, and he was locked up in a cryptlike cell in the city jail on St. Andrew's Hill, where the flint walls were so tightly constructed "as scarcely to admit the edge of a knife between the joints." There was no escape—and yet still the man would not talk.

On October 21, smoke and fire came pouring into the building: the city block was in flames. Inmates and guards alike rushed out into the street, but one prisoner proved particularly hard to rescue. *Gentleman's Magazine* marveled at him the following week: "[He] was with difficulty got away, seeming more to wonder at the fire, than to apprehend any danger, and would probably have perished like a horse in the flames." The animal-like behavior seemed fitting enough, though. "By his behavior," the writer continued, "and his want of Speech, he seems to be more of the *Ouran-Outang* species than of human."

The comparison was not entirely fanciful. The Scottish judge James Burnett, better known by his title Lord Monboddo, had been thinking a great deal about men and orangutans. Monboddo was already well-known for his eccentric insistence on following the example of the Greeks and Romans—ours was a degenerate age, he explained, and theirs was heroic and worthy of emulation. Monboddo promoted such farcical ancient ideas as bathing every day, drinking plenty of water, and getting lots of fresh air, as well as applying oils to preserve the luster of the skin. Monboddo's pungent countrymen thought their sweet-smelling judge was out of his mind.

But Monboddo was a popular member of respectable society, mixing readily with literati on his visits to London and regularly hosting the philosopher David Hume and the economist Adam Smith at suppers at his Edinburgh home. Back on his ancestral estate in the countryside, Monboddo would toss aside his formal clothing for the garments of a country farmer, a habit his peers found bizarre. It was here that he was visited by Samuel Johnson and the ever-present Boswell. "Monboddo [Estate]," Boswell recalled, "is a wretched place, wild and naked, with a poor house." But Monboddo, greeting them in a farmer's outfit, was unrepentant about his rude home.

"In such houses our ancestors lived, who were better men than we," he explained to Johnson.

"No, no, my Lord," Johnson shot back. "We are as strong as they, and a good deal wiser."

Boswell half expected the two men to come to blows. Instead, Monboddo invited them in for a simple country dinner. Johnson and Boswell found their host's sudden rusticity a bit ludicrous, but Monboddo took his responsibility as a farmer quite seriously, for being in close touch with nature was crucial to understanding man in his pure state. Johnson and Monboddo soon got into another argument at the table: Who had the better existence, a London shopkeeper or a savage? Johnson, typically, insisted on the Londoner. And Monboddo, as always, insisted on the noble and uncorrupted savage.

So it was no great surprise, in June 1782, when the aging Scottish judge sauntered up to the Fenn farmhouse outside Berkhamsted. Monboddo had been collecting accounts of feral children for years, convinced that they held the key to understanding the noble primitive state of humanity. Now, at last, he would meet the most famous feral child of them all.

Peter wasn't a child anymore, of course—he was a bearded old fellow reckoned to be seventy and had learned over the years to become rather fond of gin. He was brought out to meet Monboddo, the metal tag on his leather collar rattling slightly. The Fenns had it made for Peter decades earlier, after his adventure in Norwich, and it was inscribed:

Peter the Wild Boy
Broadway Farm, Berkhampstead

Fittingly enough, after he'd been rescued from Norwich, a pub next door to the jail took the name The Wild Boy.

Despite his age, the wild boy struck the old judge as having "a fresh, healthy look." And *Homo ferus* certainly sounded much the same as when he had arrived on the farm over fifty years earlier:

"Who are you?"

"Wild Man."

"Where were you found?"

"Hanover."

"Who is your father?"

"King George."

"What is your name?"

This was a little harder for him, and there was a pause in the word as he said it.

"Pe-ter."

A dog was pointed at.

"What is that?"

"Bow-wow."

He was then asked to name the family horse.

"Cuckow."

This was always Peter's answer to this question, even though there was no horse on the farm by that name. It was his own word. Indeed, when asked to count to twenty, the wild boy would do so correctly on his fingers, but accompanied with what sounded like his own words for the numbers. "But after another person," Monboddo puzzled, "he will say one, two, three, &c., pretty distinctly."

He understands everything he hears, the mistress assured Monboddo. And he could sing, too: he loved songs and would rattle his collar tag in joy when music was played. He could even sing, in a

rough and strange way, and the wild boy was coaxed into a popular
song for the visiting lord:

> *Of all the girls in our town,*
> *The red, the black, the fair, the brown,*
> *That dance and prance it up and down,*
> *There's none like Nancy Dawson . . .*

And then, when the song was over and the catechism of simple
questions exhausted, the old man fell silent and would not say
anything more.

Monboddo left, puzzling over what he had seen, and was a few
miles out of town when one last question seized him. He turned and
rode back to the farm and took aside Peter's keepers "to ask whether
he had ever betrayed any sense of a Supreme Being."

No, he was told.

Monboddo pondered this wild boy's simple and godless existence as
he wrote a second volume of his six-part magnum opus of natural
philosophy, the quaintly titled *Antient Metaphysics*. When the new
volume appeared later that year, readers found much of the book's first
chapter devoted to Peter's case. Peter was, Monboddo theorized, "a
living example of the state of Nature . . . In this state I think every
nation in the world must have been at some time or another." In this
state of pure nature, man was scarcely any different from the other
animals, because, he explained, man *was* an animal. Yanking the Great
Chain of Being in this way was risky, but Monboddo went even further.
Not only was man an animal, but he was *descended* from animals.
Monboddo believed that the recently discovered orangutans of Africa
were but "a step in this progression," citing travelers' reports of
specimens that had raided settlements for human wives and who

had then had children by them—proof positive that orangutans were simply a hairy and wordless form of man. Man was barely removed from being an intelligent but wordless primate, and Peter the Wild Boy was Monboddo's living proof—his missing link.

The book was not well received. The notion was so ludicrous, so out of the range of thinkable thoughts, that rather than angrily suppressing Monboddo's ideas, people laughed at them. It didn't help that Monboddo insisted that humans themselves had once possessed tails—and that in some far-off lands, such people still existed. "There are men with tails," Monboddo insisted. "There are many, I know, who will not believe that such men exist, for the same reason that they will not believe that the Ouran Outan is a man."

Caricatures of tailed men tormenting Monboddo promptly appeared, and Samuel Johnson smugly remarked: "Other people have strange notions; but they conceal them. If they have tails they hide them; but Monboddo is as jealous of his tail as a squirrel." Monboddo's theory did have problems, as it didn't explain *how* a species might evolve over time. Even worse, Monboddo had larded his account with wild tales of races of mermaids, dog-headed men, and other fanciful creatures de-scribed in classic authors. His reverence for the Greeks and Romans had led him terribly astray.

In his more paranoid moments, Monboddo suspected that mid-wives were secretly cutting the tails off infants, the better to hide the true relation of monkey to man. And the wild boy, he insisted in a letter to a friend who had also visited Peter, surely should have "enlarged your ideas of our species . . . [with] a truer knowledge of it than is to be acquired from all the modern books put together, that have been written on the subject." Monboddo went to his grave in

1799 certain that he was right. The world would have to wait another lifetime for their Darwin.

If Monboddo was pelted with ridicule in Britain, one scholar in Europe followed his work on Peter and orangutans closely. Though only thirty years old in 1782, Johann Blumenbach had been a professor of medicine for years at Monboddo's alma mater, the University of Göttingen. But whereas Monboddo had faded into obscurity, as the decades passed Blumenbach's reputation rose with the publication of the continent's standard textbooks of physiology. He made voyages to London, and the prince regent was so impressed with the eminent doctor that he appointed Blumenbach royal physician to the family back in Hanover—a title not so different from that once held by Dr. Arbuthnot. Like his predecessor, he found himself drawn to the case of the enigmatic wild boy of Hamelin.

In 1811, a full eighty-five years since the first Peter pamphlet had been published to hawk a cure for the clap, Blumenbach entered the fray with his own booklet, published in German in Göttingen. Peter's story had by now passed into history, for the wild boy and everyone who had known him were long gone. But Blumenbach's sleuthing held one great advantage over Monboddo and such eminent predecessors as Defoe, Swift, Rousseau, and Linnaeus. In all their fuss over the wild boy's appearance in the royal court in London, no one thought to go to the continent and make inquiries in Hamelin.

Examining the town's records, the doctor discovered a trove of local chronicles, including an account by Burgomeister Severin, the man who had first taken Peter in. Blumenbach found that town officials had quietly concluded that their young charge was, in fact, the son of a widower named Kruger, who lived in the nearby village of Luchtringen. The widower's unfathomably strange child—not an idiot and yet somehow not quite *right*—had run away into the woods in 1723 and roamed far afield. "[He] had been found again in the following year, quite in a different place," Blumenbach wrote. "But meanwhile his father had remarried a second time." This new stepmother quickly thrust young Kruger out of their house—not for anything that he had done, it was said, but for what he would *not* do.

The boy refused to speak.

CHAPTER 4

So they push a folder full of papers across the dining room table at us. It's nearly half an hour since we started, and we're only now getting to the evaluation results: everything so far has been review this document, sign that form, keep this guide for your reference later. The last time I remember such a barrage of paper was when we got our mortgage. Only these are not bankers. Mindy is an early intervention specialist, and Mary Jo is a speech pathologist.

"First of all"—Mary Jo opens the folder as Jennifer and I look over one last form to sign—"no one number is going to provide you with a conclusion. What we look for is a *pattern*, a tendency for certain behaviors and skills to cluster together."

We nod obediently. We will not jump to any conclusions based on any one number. Anyway, I probably signed a form promising to be reasonable.

"Here's the developmental history—let me know if we've got any facts wrong . . ."

She begins reciting from the first page as I skim through the text: "Paul was evaluated as a child for possible hearing impairment. So Morgan's selective responses to sounds and words as well as limited language seemed a familiar pattern. Parents report normal developmental milestones with the exception of communication."

"Paul?" Jennifer says.

"Hmm?"

Mindy hands us another set of papers. "Now here are the evaluation results." She turns the page.

The results are split into an array of development: cognitive, social, emotional, adaptive sensory assessment, and so on. It is for the kinds of things that, before you become a parent, you don't even realize that you yourself had to learn once—Do you use words to make requests? Do you respond to your name? Can you recognize a square versus a circle? When someone plays next to you, will you join them? Can you tie your shoes? . . . My God. How did we learn this stuff? How on earth do we keep track of it all? How did primates get from pushing sticks into anthills to this?

"Now," Mindy says, "Morgan showed exceptional cognitive skills for age three. His skills are those normally associated with forty-eight and sixty months, and some appear even beyond that . . ."

He counts. He reads. He thinks. He *knows*.

"But here in the noncognitive areas of social, sensory, and receptive, and expressive communication, we start seeing different scores. Diadic is nine to twelve months, over here we see eighteen months . . ."

Nine months? I turn page after page: 1 percent; 1 percent; 3 percent; 1 percent.

What?

"These scores are *percentiles* comparing him to other three-year-olds," Mindy tells us patiently. "That's not the same as a *percentage*. What a percentile means is . . ." But I stop listening and stare at the numbers.

I know what percentiles are. I know what a percentile means.

*   *   *

The evaluation papers have been sitting there on the dining table for weeks. I can't even look at them again. I finally push them aside so that I can empty out the old wooden cabinet that we have haphazardly stuffed with thick one-hour photo envelopes. I start selecting snapshots: Morgan playing a set of drums in his pajamas; Morgan in his Tigger costume; Morgan riding in his little red wagon; Morgan soaking himself with a green garden hose; Morgan singing as he plays piano. I slide each picture into a translucent green photo wallet that I bought for the trip.

Jennifer pauses as she walks past me.

"I like that one, on top," she says, and walks on into the kitchen. It's of me holding Morgan and tickling him while he giggles with delight.

"Me too." I put it into the wallet. "I don't know. Should I even be going?"

She takes out the sugar and shortening to start on a loaf of banana bread. "Honey, the taxi'll be on its way soon."

"I feel kind of bad going on a research trip now. I mean, with everything going on."

"You planned it months ago. We didn't know back then."

"Yeah."

She wipes her hands and holds me from behind the chair. "You should go. Seriously. Marc's here. We'll be fine. It's only a week."

I look over at my single schoolbag waiting by the door, crammed with clothes and research notes, at the ready for the red-eye flight out of Portland.

"I know," I finally say. "You're right."

Morgan barrels through the front door, with Marc following behind him.

"How'd it go?"

"We fed the ducks at the park," Marc reports. "And then he tried to join them in the pond."

"Ah."

Morgan scrambles up into my lap and looks over the glossy photos on the table. He guides my finger to one of them.

"That's you, Morgan. That's you opening your birthday presents."

He jabs my finger at another.

"That's you, too! That's Morgan and Daddy reading a book."

He springs back off my lap and jumps onto the chair in front of his computer, where *Maisy's Playhouse* has been left on pause. He clicks it back to life and focuses intensely. But he stops occasionally to move his chair to one side, then the other, then back again. I watch as he drags one and then two chairs from the dining table to his computer and then tosses in a small step stool for good measure. He lines them all up in front of the computer and hops back and forth delightedly, from one chair to the other, playing his game all the while.

Inevitably, a taxi beeps outside. I hug my son as he plays and then cup his chin and try to turn his head.

"Morgan? . . . Morgan?"

He is staring into his game.

"Morgan. Look at Daddy, sweetie. Morgan . . . Mor-gan?"

He glances over at me.

"You're my little man. You're my little guy. I love you."

He leans against me wordlessly, content, and keeps playing. And when I slip out the front door, he is still absorbed in his computer. He does not hear me leave.

"Round trip to Berkhamsted, please."

"Pardon?" the ticket agent says.

"Rou—" I stop. I've momentarily forgotten where I am. "*Cheap day return* to Berkhamsted."

"Eight pounds ten."

I fish the money out of my wallet, and the morning's accumulated slips of paper flutter from my pocket: underground tickets, a scrap with an address and time scrawled on it, and a ticket into Kensington Palace, where I ignored the taped audio guides and rushed around clots of tourists and past room after baroque room, just so I could gawk at one painting in a stairway.

"One pound ninety change." She pushes forward my tickets and coins. "Next train departs at one oh-three."

I stuff everything back into my pockets.

"Thanks." I grab a *Guardian* and an Aero bar before jogging through the white-tiled expanse to my train. Euston was a great Victorian station once, with a massive Doric arch at its entrance; but that was all torn down in the 1960s for a modern concrete structure. Progress.

The Berkhamsted train scarcely takes me outside of London, clicking rather lazily over the trestles for all of forty minutes. But it feels far away, and after the train ambles off I am left alone on the little platform. I still have to hike a good half hour from the station, so I sling my schoolbag over my shoulder and set off.

The sun is shining, a March breeze is blowing through the hedges, and the occasional car driving on the wrong side of the road roars past. Far behind me I can still hear the rattle of the London-to-Birmingham line. The path inclines, and I root through my bag: I haven't brought water. Ah, well. I scuff little bits of flinted stones underfoot and walk on. The buildings of town gradually thin out, and trees begin to shade the way.

MONTAGUE PIANOS reads a sign over the old house at a curve in the road up ahead. I listen intently, thinking I'll hear someone plonking out "Chopsticks" or "Candle in the Wind," but no, nothing. There is no sound here, no traffic even. Just wind. I'm in Northchurch now, I suppose, a little village fragmented from Berkhamsted proper. It is a quiet place, especially on a Wednesday afternoon. I stop and look around. How, I wonder, did this place look—back then?

Up past the curve, I can begin to see my destination. It is the same walk the villagers have made for a thousand years now. I cross the street from the George and Dragon pub and walk down a church-yard path awash in budding daffodils: it carves its way through a rise in the ground, a green expanse of grass and worn and leaning tombstones, gently leading down into a little hollow.

I try a massive wooden door. Locked. So I knock. Nothing. I knock again, then walk backward and look up at the rocky hulk of a church towering over me.

"Hello?" I yell.

The wind rustles the daffodils.

"Hell-ooo?"

I must be at the wrong door. I walk around the church, admiring its massive and gorgeous walls—built in the Hertfordshire style from squared-off chunks of flint, like the jail that once held their wild boy. This is the new part of the old church, new meaning fifteenth century; the original section is eleventh century. I suppose that was new once, too; God only knows how long there was a church standing here before that one.

There is a side door, even more impossibly old looking than the first one.

"Hello? Reverend? . . . Hello?"

I am alone.

He must live nearby—these reverends don't actually live in the church, do they? I mean, imagine the heating bill—he must be in a house next door. But next door is a schoolhouse, shut up for the spring break; next to that, a modest little wooden building. Ah, surely this is the dwelling of a man of God.

"Hello? Reverend?" I peer in through a dirty window.

It's a toolshed.

"Trying to find Reverend Hart?"

I look up; a woman at the next house over is hanging laundry in her yard.

"Yes, yes, I am."

"You'll be wanting to go that way." She points across the churchyard.

"Of course. Thanks."

I walk back through the rows of graves and—*hallo!*—spot a man coming up a pathway. I glance at my watch: I'm not late yet, which is good, since standing up a man of the cloth is liable to earn me an extra hour on the divine griddle someday.

We shake hands. I was expecting a stooped old man in a little village like this, but he looks about the same age as me—and is nearly a ringer, in fact, for the British actor Timothy Spall.

"So," he says. "You're looking for the wild boy."

He sets the burial register on a pew and leafs through it. It is cool and dark here in the nave of the unlit church; a little light filters in through the stained glass.

"Let's see, 1785, 1785 . . ." The reverend runs his finger along the columns. "Ah. Here we are. 'Peter—Commonly Call'd the Wild Boy.' Buried February 27, 1785. Hmm."

"What?"

"Five days after he died. Usually they buried them within a couple of days."

"That's odd."

"An unusual fellow all around. The tablet to him is behind you."

He points to the south wall of the nave, the oldest part of the church, where the wall is a thousand years old. A brass plaque was bolted into the flint two hundred years ago and is barely visible in the darkness:

> To the memory of PETER known by the name of the Wild Boy, having been found Wild in the Forest of Hertswold near Hanover in the year 1725: he then appeared to be about 12 years old. In the year following he was brought to England by the order of the late Queen Caroline, and the ablest masters were provided for him. But proving incapable of speaking or of receiving any instruction a comfortable provision was made for him by her Majesty at a farm house in this Parish, where he continued to the end of his inoffensive life. He died on 22nd day of February 1785, supposed to be Aged 72.

I look down at the floor beneath the tablet.

"Is this where he's buried?" I nod at the flagstones.

"You didn't see the grave?"

"No. Is it easy to find?"

Reverend Hart beckons me to follow him and points through the heavy transept door that parishioners walk through as they leave the service.

"There."

The pathway leading into the church is cut so deeply into the ground that the churchyard is very nearly level with one's head, so my eyes meet it directly: a mossy old stone beneath an overgrown bush.

PETER

the Wild Boy

1785.

I stare at the words for a long time. I have found him at last.

"The library closes in one hour. Please make your final book requests."

My stomach is growling. I haven't eaten anything since the candy bar at the rail station, hours ago. But it's closing time soon: I have to read faster, concentrate. It's not as if the rare-book room at the British Library is a place where you can get comfortable. No pens allowed, no bags, no water bottles, no nothing: just you and the books. I look up from mine a lot, across rows and rows of scholars, all perusing priceless volumes at identical rows of burnished tables and lamps. Nobody else looks up from their work but me.

I have my own stacks of books, everything from Pope's and Defoe's pamphlets and thick volumes of *Gentleman's Magazine* to Monboddo's weighty volumes of ill-fated evolutionary theory. It's all in here, all hidden away. I also have a few modern books that I've scarcely bothered with yet. For no good reason, I pick one up, by anthropologist Werner Stark. He has a brief section on feral children, but it was written when Stark was well into retirement, and it has the feel of an old man's rambling conversation. I am about to toss it back into the pile when a word catches my eye.

I read the sentence again and then again.

"Twenty minutes to closing," comes the announcement.

I never knew *why* I had wanted to write about Peter the Wild Boy. I'd become interested a little before Morgan turned two. Peter seemed like a curious but forgotten case, a man whom no one had written a book about in two hundred years. But long before going to the doctor, before the batteries of tests on Morgan, before the diagnosis, before we ever imagined anything—I had been chasing a silent boy through the even greater silence of centuries, when my own boy was in front of me all along. How? How could I not have seen it? *Something* drew me to Peter, something so obvious now that Stark barely mentions it in passing in his book:

An early case of autism.

PART TWO

FALLEN FROM THE SKY

CHAPTER 5

There's a terrible cold snap in Vienna when I arrive on my flight from London; by the time I reach the city from the airport, the freezing morning fog that left white rime on the trees has been replaced by blowing flurries of snow. I can feel the wind rushing by outside the tram window as we rattle past the Staatsoper.

"You like that building?" asks an old woman in the seat next to mine, nodding at the opera house. I look over at it; it is, like every other building chunking up alongside Kärtner Ring, a blocky rockpile of Austro-empiric wealth. You could render central Vienna pretty well using nothing but cream-colored Legos. Only the opera house is a little different; its old upper arches have been glassed in with the spidery angularity of modern bay windows.

"I think it's ugly," she spits. "They should leave the old buildings alone."

I nod and look around at the other passengers in the tram. They are minding their own business, listening to headphones and staring out the windows. The tram, at least, has never really changed. If you dressed these students and pensioners a little differently, you could imagine it was many decades ago. The interior of the tram is worn and polished wood and metal, like old schoolhouse desks, the same as seventy years ago. The same scrape of metal wheels on rail, the same blowing snow, the endless parade of monumental buildings drifting by, the same sleepy litany of tram stops announced by the conductor: Karlsplatz . . . Mariahilferstrasse . . .

Volkstheater . . .

My eyelids get heavy.

Lerchenfelderstrasse . . .

I bolt up from my seat, grab my backpack, and tap a button to open the side door. Cold air blasts in as I step out, and I rub my eyes with my gloves as the wind freezes my cheeks. Then the tram clatters away and I am alone.

"Burggasse . . ." I fumble for the slip of paper. I can't read my own writing from my last-minute notes, made as my trip plans suddenly transformed from the trail of one mysterious child to the trail of an entire tribe of myterious children. "Burggasse 88."

I make my way over to Burggasse and past the U-Bahn station entrance; warm air is blowing out alluringly, but I continue onward and hug myself against the cold. It's Sunday in a Catholic country. Everything is quiet and closed: the piano shop where they display various mechanical innards in the window, the old bookstores, the musty antique shops. I stop and look up and then check again. Yes. Burggasse 88.

It's an unassuming old three-story walk-up like any other on the street; a small pair of brass plates announce that upstairs are the offices of SciCon and HumanWare. The ground floor is decidedly less futuristic: a dusty scavenger's shop, its storefront window a melancholy diorama of old printer's-type trays, horseshoes, and glass patent medicine bottles. Another window is filled with vintage sheet music: heaps of yellowing novelty tunes and Strauss waltzes. I lean in at the darkened window to read the title on an aging sheet tucked in an upper corner. "Ja, Ja, der Wein is Gut."

Below it are sheets of *Wiener Kinder* series music for children, from many decades ago. I stand back in the empty street and look up at the building. What was it like to walk up this building, back then, when it was a children's clinic? In the 1930s, some of the Austrian children playing *Wiener Kinder* music would have been playing it in this very building, to assembled knots of doctors, nurses, and interns. It was easy enough for the children to get here: Then, as now, Vienna had Europe's most elaborate tram system. But on the way over, on freezing days such as this, some of the young children were not simply staring out the tram windows at the Parliament building or the Rathaus. No, this was the curious thing, the unsettling thing. Some of them were memorizing the Vienna tram schedules.

Fritz W. was one of the early cases. They showed the boy a picture of a fly and a butterfly and asked: what is the difference between the two?

"Because he has a different name."

Come again?

"Because," the boy explained, "the butterfly is snowed, snowed with snow."

A different question: why are wood and glass different?

"Because the glass is more glassy and the wood more woody."

A cow and a calf: what is the difference?

"Lammerlammerlammer . . ."

He would not look at them, would not answer the question.

". . . lammerlammerlammerlammer . . ."

Try again: "Which is the bigger one?"

"The cow I would like to have the pen now."

Fritz had come into the University of Vienna Pediatric Clinic in the fall of 1939, a six-year-old classified by his teachers as "ineducable." The clinic at 88 Burggasse was as good a place as any for him: there, placed into a daily routine of learning and play under the governess Sister Viktorine Zak, he could be observed by the young resident doctors who were training to be the future of European pediatric science.

But what was there to observe in young Fritz, exactly? He did not respond to his name; did not respond, in fact, to any sort of command at all. Ask him a question, and he'd repeat a random word of it back at you, deadpan, without meaning—drawn out in a low, mock adult voice or simply mocking in a singsong voice. He never looked his questioners in the eye when he responded; he scarcely seemed to take any notice of the people around him at all and would talk into empty space. He ran about clumsily, he shrieked, he jumped up and down on the beds; give him a pencil and paper, and he would eat both in their entirety.

He was also remarkably good at doing fractions.

How? It was a question that vexed one young doctor in training, Hans Asperger. There had been a strange abundance of such boys coming into the clinic . . . and they were almost always boys. Boys of an unbreakable and all-consuming focus on random minutiae, who memorized tram lines and calendars, who obsessively collected bits of thread and matchboxes, who would not play with other children but would endlessly arrange toys into orderly straight lines across the floor. These were boys who could read far ahead of their years but not talk, who could calculate brilliantly but not dress or bathe themselves. Lost in abstraction, they had, Asperger mused, "a helplessness in matters of practical life typical of the absent-minded professor."

One such boy, the doctor wrote, acted "as if he had just fallen from the sky."

* * *

It's only a short ride from the clinic to the university, and when I step off the tram, I crane my head up: Snowflakes fall on my cheeks as I eye the great building across the street. It is covered in scaffolding; they are scrubbing away the brown grime of city life to reveal the whitish stone underneath, so that soon one can forget that time or decay had ever touched the place, that generations of men now dead passed through it. A sharp wind rips through my coat as I cross Wahringerstrasse; a student is outside, clapping her mittens for warmth, and a couple of others shelter beneath the scaffolding from the blowing snow. The university is a solid block of building, circumscribing a central courtyard: a singular structure, not like the sprawling, disconnected campuses of the modern day. The building is a monolith with only a few ways in or out.

A door opens into a gloomy hall of arches leading into the peaceful courtyard, but I halt in the entranceway. I suppose they all passed through this very spot. This entranceway is the lens of Viennese culture; the convergent point where light entering splits off into all directions. And so it is, by strange chance, that four men passed through, each destined to illuminate the curious cases at the university clinic. One cast his light as far as Asperger's was near. Unknown to Asperger as he pondered his cases down the road from this university, another Viennese alum was in far-off Baltimore, musing over the same symptoms.

"Since 1938," his report began, "there have come to our attention a number of children whose condition differs so markedly and uniquely from anything reported so far, that each case merits—and I hope will eventually receive—a detailed consideration of its fascinating peculiarities."

These, the opening lines of Dr. Leo Kanner's 1943 paper "Autistic Disturbances of Affective Contact," were the first in English about the condition that had manifested itself in the Johns Hopkins University clinic where Kanner worked since emigrating from Vienna in 1922. Kanner described eleven cases of boys who seemed lost and aloof, unable to speak or move normally, and obsessed with repetition and arrangement of objects. They were unable to handle simple pronouns—reversing "I" and "you" seemed to be universal among them—yet they could also be *hyperlexic*, endlessly paging through books. Describing a boy named Donald, Kanner marveled at how his symptoms were immediately apparent: "An invitation to enter the office was disregarded but he led himself willingly. Once inside, he did not even glance at the three physicians present . . . but immediately made for the desk and handled the papers and books."

Kanner coined the word *autism* to describe their condition, and his paper founded the field of autistic study. But unknown to Kanner, at his old school in Vienna, Hans Asperger had just submitted a thesis on the same disorder. In one of those odd quirks of history, the total lack of communication between the warring countries meant that both had made their discoveries independently and simultaneously. Incredibly, they had also chosen the same word to describe it.

"The *autist* is only himself (cf. the Greek word *autos*) and is not a member of the greater organism," Asperger explained in his 1943 thesis. Like Kanner, Asperger had heard the same description from the children's parents and teachers: *it's as if he's in his own world*. And like Kanner, Asperger had seen these boys so often that he developed a sixth sense of them: "Once one has properly recognized an autistic individual one can spot such children instantly . . . [from] the way they enter the consulting room at their first visit, their behavior in the first moments and the first words they utter."

They simply did not *get* human interaction in the effortless way that the rest of us do instinctively, and from the moment of the first and most basic social cue—saying hello, but not getting a response—these children were marked as outsiders. Their inability to meet a gaze, the way they nervously flapped their hands, their flat and stilted speaking, their frenzied fits of frustration, their inability to grasp basic social cues, their endless repetitions of phrases and words—any one such trait was merely a quirk or an eccentricity, but to see the same constellation of traits over and over again meant there was something more.

"From the second year of life," Asperger observed, "we find already the characteristic features which remain unmistakable and constant throughout the *whole* life-span." It was a condition far beyond the realm of talking cures and educational bromides, for these children were fundamentally and permanently different from any others. Yet Asperger's charges were capable of feats of almost incredible brilliance. They could be inept to the point of retardation at the simplest question-answer exercises or at feeding themselves; yet at least one was doing cubic root calculations before kindergarten, and another was memorizing masses of information on rockets. But they could not respond when asked for their own names.

Asperger alone sensed that this might be the root of savantism, that most mysterious of cognitive oddities. Prodigies able to calculate endless strings of numbers, to identify the day of the week from any date over a span of centuries, or to produce virtuosic musical performances from the depths of imbecility—this had been the stuff of popular wonder for centuries. What Asperger had discovered in his Vienna clinic was the greater tribe from which these most spectacular examples had sprung.

Punished by teachers and tormented by other children, talented autists could retreat into a world of intense cognition. Others—

children with no special abilities, with retardation atop their profound otherness—were not so fortunate. And both alike faced the same gauntlet, each day, of an illogical world that not only made no sense to them, but hated them for it. "In the playground or on the way to school one can often see an autistic child at the center of a jeering horde of little urchins. The child himself may be hitting out in blind fury or crying helplessly," Asperger warned grimly. "In either case, he is defenseless."

Their treatment by children was bad; the adults were even worse. With Nazi eugenics at its genocidal peak, clinics and households were being emptied of "defectives," and Asperger faced the real possibility that his patients might be murdered almost before his eyes. And while Kanner's work became famous, Asperger's was buried when the massive 1944 Allied bombing of Vienna came crashing into the university pediatric clinic. Asperger survived. But his discoveries, his carefully run ward, and even the supremely capable governess Sister Viktorine—all perished.

I ring the doorbell tentatively and wait in the dark stairwell. It creaks open slowly to a brightly lit room and a young woman who might have, like myself, just walked over here from the university campus.

"*Ja,*" she says, and instantly sizes up my nationality. "Come in."

I step into the front parlor of Dr. Freud.

"You may put your coat in this closet"—she indicates—"and enter the household through that doorway."

I have been trying to catch up with Freud all day; earlier I took my breakfast in the café down the street where he ate every morning. I was nearly alone in the place. After asking a waitress where he used to sit—"*Ich weiss nicht,*" she said with a shrug—I sat by a window. Good for observing people, I decided.

There is nobody else here, either; the museum is not a busy place. You really are visiting someone's apartment: the address where Freud spent most of his life is on the second floor of a walk-up in an old and rather well-hidden building. You slip past the front gate, stroll through the courtyard and past other apartments still in use by the living, and climb the apartment stairwell until you see the door: DR. FREUD. He might as well still be alive; it is as if you are visiting the doctor himself as yet another of his afternoon appointments.

I wander through Freud's house until I find myself in his old waiting room, where framed degrees hang on the wall. The couches are respectable Victorians, a little oppressive in the dim light. It is the sort of room in which one hears the ticking of an old clock on the mantel—even if there is not, in actuality, a clock or a mantel anywhere to be found. I look out the window into his courtyard, clasp my hands behind my back, and rock back and forth on my toes impatiently. I don't suppose he'll be keeping the appointment.

The traces of Kanner and Asperger are gone in Vienna, but those of their more famous university colleague remain; there is at least this one preserved residence of the city's intellectual past, the passages and doorways that one may follow down and through, taking the steps of the ghosts of doctors and patients past. It was in these rooms that the Gestapo rifled through Freud's belongings; and these rooms that Freud had to abandon when he fled Vienna in 1938, just ahead of the tidal wave that drowned much of the city's intelligentsia. Not everyone escaped, at least not for a while—and among those who were left behind was a self-proclaimed protégé who was to have an extraordinary impact in the field of autism. Freud couldn't have known it back then; he would not even have recognized the student that his household so famously mentored.

* * *

The picture is a striking one: you can still find it in some old copies of the book. In it, a little girl named Laurie is quietly engrossed in creating a sine-wave border out of tanbark, arranged with remarkable precision down a concrete verge. It is her obsession. Another photo shows her clever solution to maintaining her sine-wave pattern around a right-angled corner in the verge:

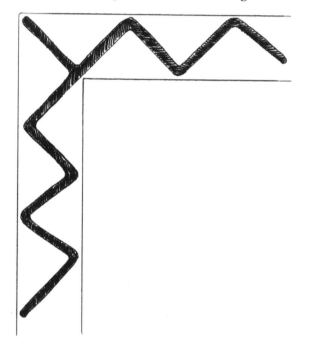

The concrete verge was outside the Orthogenic School at the University of Chicago. Inside was Bruno Bettelheim, the Viennese doctor who had risen to the top of his profession by overseeing autistic children like Laurie at the school. Bettelheim seemed to have come from out of nowhere upon the wartime refugee wave of Jewish intellectuals, but like his colleagues Kanner and Asperger, he could boast of a string of degrees and clinical training in Vienna. The University of Chicago was only too glad to hand over a ward full of intractable cases to him: Nobody knew what to do with a girl like Laurie. She had come to the school at the age of seven in an emaciated state, "completely inert," after not having spoken a single word in four years. Laurie could not feed or dress herself; she dribbled vomit over her clothes.

Hers was by no means the only dire case. There was also the girl who sat all day in bed, rocking back and forth in a yoga position, covering her ears and eyes with her hands, and pushing away all physical contact. In another bed was the cyborg-boy, who strung around his bedposts a maniacally fantastic contraption of cardboard, wire, and tape—a "car-machine" that kept him alive, with a carburetor for breathing and motors for his digestion. He liked to draw pictures of men whose bodies consisted of electric wiring.

What these children had in common, Bettelheim explained, was that their "only means of asserting independence had been to deny all validity of the external world through autistic withdrawal." These young unfortunates—Laurie, Marcia, and Joey—also had something else in common, for their three case studies were the core of Bettelheim's 1967 book, *The Empty Fortress*. Bettelheim described how he and his staff had drawn each child out of their autistic shell—a protective shell, he asserted, created by a toxic combination of uncaring parents and a primal shock in early childhood. One autistic child's illness was rooted in the trauma of his parents leaving a bedroom window open on a cold night. Laurie, it was decided after she started administering enemas to one of her dolls, was traumatized by enemas given during an infant bout of constipation. But by careful Freudian decoding of the mysterious puns uttered by these enigmatic children—Marcia's fascination with weather was decrypted as a threat of "we eat her"—they could be coaxed, slowly, back into the world.

Above all else, Bettelheim implied, it was necessary to get these children away from their homes. When Laurie was snatched away by her thoughtless parents, she declined back into a near vegetative state at a state hospital. Bettelheim wrote wrenchingly of visiting her, explaining to her that he wished she could have stayed with him. Out of her profound silence, "she turned her head, looking into my face with eyes that suggested some understanding, and laid her hand on my knee." But then Bettelheim has to explain that he can't free her from the hospital her parents have put her into. "She slowly withdrew her hand, and though I stayed for another while there was no more flicker of response or recognition." Bettelheim, himself a survivor of the Dachau and Buchenwald concentration camps, could not help but wonder in his book whether the resignation he had seen in his fellow prisoners was not unlike what he saw in these children.

A HERO FOR OUR TIME one review in *The New Republic* was headlined; *The New Yorker* hailed Bettelheim's "spectacular successes" and grieved over pathological families that had been "efficient machines for dehumanization—little, unwitting concentration camps." Soon Bettelheim was everywhere. His work was excerpted in *The New York Times Magazine*, and the doctor himself appeared on the *Today* show. He was the media's popular introduction to this exotic disorder, and art thrived on the notion of mysteriously withdrawn children suffering from a secret primal hurt. Soon after the book's release, The Who built their rock opera *Tommy* around a boy whose childhood trauma turns him into a profoundly autistic savant—a deaf-and-dumb pinball wizard. And it was Bettelheim's book that first hazarded the provocative guess that feral "wolf children" had been autistic, too strange for their parents to cope with, but intelligent enough to survive in the wild.

Bettelheim became one of the most widely read psychologists

alive, the worthy heir to the fame of his old mentor, Freud. His work was wielded by social workers certain that autistic children needed to be removed from the "refrigerator mothers" who had ruined them. Families were broken up and children institutionalized—for their own good, of course. Yet there were some curious lapses in Bettelheim's theory. For one thing, many of the households in question did not, at first glance, much resemble Dachau. Moreover, these autistic children had siblings who appeared perfectly normal. Why hadn't their sadistic mothers made them autistic, too?

"Excuse me, wh—" I start to a passerby, and correct myself. "*Wie spät ist—*"

"Almost five," he says in English.

"Thanks."

The sun is starting to set, and snow is still flurrying over the expanse of Sigmund Freud Park. Across the field I can see the university building and the tram gliding by. The university is so wonderfully compact. It wouldn't have taken much. One sheet of paper, one airmail stamp. One inquiry to this campus: it might not even have required that, for an investigator within the walls of the Orthogenic School would have found that the published case studies did not quite match the patients there. Nor would they have found the miraculous cures that Bettelheim was famous for; the very existence of some of these children was an open question. But through a half-open door, an observer would have seen "Dr. B" punching and slapping his disabled patients. And if they had looked even closer into his records, they would have noticed something else.

Bettelheim was not a doctor.

CHAPTER 6

They don't know what to do with him.

Jennifer signs in at the front desk—"Speech development?" she explains to a receptionist holding a clipboard. "I don't know why, but they put us into speech development."

I kneel down next to Morgan at a lobby table scattered with toys. He is playing with a block-and-peg set.

"Triangle," I tell him. "That's a triangle peg."

He knows what it is: he pushes me away dismissively.

I put my arm around him and look around. I still feel woozy with jet lag. The building that houses this part of the early intervention program used to be a nursing home for the elderly, and it's all one floor: no elevators, lots of bathrooms. I suppose that people used to die here.

A pair of angelic four-year-old girls look cautiously into the lobby. Bruce rolls up his wheelchair behind them, case file in his lap: COLLINS.

"Caitlin, can you take Morgan's hand?"

A shy four-year-old girl grabs Morgan's little hand. He pulls it away.

"Ashley, can you take the other?"

He pulls it away.

And we all sit around him for a moment in the linoleumed lobby: me, him, Jennifer, two confused little girls, a teacher in a wheelchair.

"Ashley, Caitlin," Bruce says, "can you *both* take his hands and walk him to the classroom?"

They try: he pulls away. They look helplessly over at the teacher.

Then Morgan turns to Jennifer and grabs her hand. "Walk," he says, not looking at us.

I look over at Bruce. "Wow. I've never heard him use that word."

"Well . . ." He smiles. "That's a good start for school."

Morgan wanders around the classroom, inspecting a stack of cups, a box of sand, a little play kitchen.

"Okay . . ." Bruce lowers himself from his wheelchair onto the floor, his limp legs dangling for a perilous moment. "Let's make a circle."

The two girls obediently sit down in front of him.

"Sand," Morgan reports from the other side of the room.

"Can you sit down, Morgan? Can you come here and sit down? Can you come here and sit down?"

Morgan ignores him and inspects a cup.

"Cup," he says, though Bruce doesn't hear him.

". . . here and sit down?"

Nothing.

"Jennifer, maybe you could hold him in your lap at the circle here?"

She sits him down, and this works fine; as long as it's one of us doing the sitting with him, he's happy to sit down.

"Okay. Caitlin, can you tell me what's on this card?"

Bruce holds up a card with a picture of a cowboy.

She shakes her head.

"Caitlin," he says, "I know you can do this. I've seen you do it. What's on the card?"

"*Cow-boy*," she nearly whispers the caption.

"Say it so I can hear it."

"Cowboy."

"Very g—"

Morgan snatches the card out of Bruce's hand.

"—Ah-ha! You like the cards, Morgan? Can you give me the card? Give me the card, Morgan."

Morgan does not give him the card.

Bruce grabs it back. "Now I have the card, Morgan."

Morgan lunges out of Jennifer's lap, desperate for the cowboy card, and Bruce hands it back to him.

"Now you have the card."

Snatch.

"—And now I have the cowboy card. Who has the cowboy card?"

Morgan reaches for it, not even looking at Bruce, and Bruce holds the card over his head, monkey-in-the-middle style.

"Now *I* have the card, and"—he lowers it to the grasping child—"now *you* have the card. Who has the card, Morgan?"

Who has the card?

Who has the card?

Who—

Snatch.

"Now *I* have the card, Morgan. Can you read fr—"

Tears well up. Morgan bursts out crying, kicking and flailing. I see his little boots flying up: Jesus, he's gonna knock a girl's teeth out. But instead he leaps onto one of Bruce's legs and climbs up him for the card.

I've seen enough.

"Morgan . . ." I whisk him up as he roars. "Morgan, Morgan, it's okay, it's okay, honey, it's okay . . ."

I have to hold him facing away from me because he is screaming, his legs kicking out, stamping into the air where my ribs would be. I stroke his hair, refuse to let go; it's okay, it's okay, honey, it's . . .

The girls are staring at us.

"Why don't you play for a moment?" Bruce tells them, and they do.

He turns to us and shrugs. "This isn't the right class for him, I think."

Jennifer holds Morgan now, kisses him and dries his face.

"What is?"

"Well . . . The evaluations were calling him at the high end of the autism bell curve, but maybe he's more in the middle . . ." His hand traces out a curve in the air.

I feel my anger rising. Morgan has tantrums for a *reason*. Morgan is happy. He is happy when he is left alone, doing what he wants. It's the outside world that is the problem—outside people. *Do this, do that.* And it doesn't make sense; he cries, he flails.

"In any case, he's not ready for structured group situations yet. He needs one-on-one instruction for autistics, something to get him responding to commands and communicating with words. Until he's doing that, a group classroom doesn't make that much sense. Well, maybe for play . . ."

Morgan, tears still rolling down his cheeks, watches the girls play with some colored hoops, and he toddles over to join them. He looks at them: they look at him.

"There's imitation behavior there, that's good. And parallel play; he's not playing with the girls exactly, but he's happy to play next to them, that's a good start. But in a structured group classroom where you have to direct a group of students together—it's just not happening. Not yet."

"So we should get him into an autism classroom."

"Well . . . yes. But that class doesn't start until he's three and a half."

"He only just turned three."

"Y-esss."

"What do we do for six months?"

"I'm not sure. I need to see what the other options are for him."

Morgan has turned his attention back to the deck of cards, shuffling them down to the bottom of the deck.

"He has a thing about cards," I explain.

"Hmm." Bruce turns to him for a moment. "Can you put the cards on the *top* of the deck, Morgan? On the top?"

Morgan starts getting mad again.

"We should go." Jennifer nods at the two girls. "So you can get to—"

"I think so. I'll talk to my supervisor and call you tomorrow."

"C'mon." I pry Morgan away from the deck. "Let's go home."

There's a box waiting for us when we get to the house. Priority Mail boxes of books keep thudding onto our porch every day: *Autism. Thinking in Pictures. Understanding Other Minds. Mindblindness. The OASIS Guide. Our Journey Through Autism.* They pile up on our dining table, next to a rising stack of medical and school district paperwork.

Morgan grabs a book and examines its smooth and unwrinkled spine, rubs it against his cheek and then against his corduroy overalls; then he cranes his head and examines the edges of the pages with his eyes rolled all the way down, as if he is wearing bifocals. Hmm. Interesting, but it's no *Merck Manual*. He tosses it to the floor and climbs onto my lap to grab a Slinky off the table. He looks through it, wobbles it around, wiggles his fingers inside the coils.

"Elmo's an old cowhand," he says. Then he says it again. It's from a video that he likes: words, phrases, sometimes whole conversations come echoed back. "Elmo a-owa a-hand." He adds in syllables, subtracts them over time and over hundreds, thousands of repetitions: they become abstract phonemes, sing-songs that only he knows the lyrics to.

He cuddles against me. Spread out on the dining table are stapled printouts of medical articles and Web pages, all dug up online. First you get millions of useless hits: autism groups in Australia, in India, in Russia; autism schools; lawsuits over vaccines. Books and videos for autism. Cures for autism. Lawsuits over cures for autism. The ads are constant. Buy! Sell! Sue! Someone must pay!

. . . points.

Dred. Tee points.

I look up from the table.

"I'm sorry. What?"

"I have a hundred and twenty points," she says from across the living room.

"Ah."

Jennifer has a system for housework. She has many systems, actually. But the point system is the most important. Every item picked up, every item cleaned or moved: that is a point. Some chores, like touching up the paint on our scraped-up old wooden floors, yield damnably few points for the effort they require. But folding laundry—full of innumerable discrete objects—that is a points *bonanza*. But mostly the task of creating order simply *is*. There are jigsaw puzzles; there are crosswords; there are the enigmatic graph paper sheets of triangles arranged and colored in by a private algorithm, a different one on each sheet. She stopped making those after we moved in together, but I saved one from the recycling bin for myself. I've had it for years now, and I still can't figure out the meaning or the pattern on it.

"Did you hear me?" Jennifer says.

"Hmm?"

"Marc won't be up any time soon, since he thinks we're at school for another two hours."

"Well, Morgan's still dressed to go out . . . Hey, Morgan, do you want to go to the library with Daddy? Library? With Daddy? Go *outside* to the *library?*"

He hops down from my lap and inspects the upholstery on a chair.

"Outside?" I lead him by the hand. "Morgan?"

The air outside is cold and crisp; Morgan immediately halts and silently holds out his arms, his body forming a T. This is his signal: pick me up. I sling him up onto my shoulders, and we walk down the block to the library before I drop him back down again onto his heels. The building is a cut-rate Palladio, one of those vaguely classical brick Colonials that look like small-town banks. Where the vault would be, though, is a children's reading area. Morgan skips in flapping his coat sleeves and smiles rapturously as he looks up at the ceiling and spins around.

"Oh!"

"Shh. Shhh-shh-shh. Not so loud. It's a library, Morgan."

"Why you!" he begins to shout, and then stops. He picks a book off a table and casually reads a word he's never seen before.

"B-l-i-m-p. Blimp."

"Good job! And—"

"Why you!"

He tears off across the carpeted floor and into a bank of adults tapping at computers.

"You woe see me! You woe see me! You! Woe!"

I swoop in on him.

"Morgan, let's go read . . ."

He is a scramble of arms and legs.

"See! Me!"

Everyone is looking up, looking at me, looking at us. He bolts away from me.

"Shh-hh-shhh . . ." I chase him down across the reference section. "Morgan, come back to Daddy." But he is not looking at me. He is not looking at anyone at all.

"Why you!" he yells.

It's a phrase from a Beatles song. Everything is a phrase from somewhere: from TV, from computer games, from books, from songs. He collects broken bits of language like a magpie, gathering stray threads of conversation; and he arranges them into a nest, comfortable to him and bafflingly strange to anyone else.

"Morgan, come to Daddy . . ."

He smiles into the indeterminate distance.

"Woe see me!"

Morgan will not come to words: we must bring words to him. I go to the supermarket and buy pack after pack of neon-colored blank cards, along with an index card box normally used for recipes. Once we get home I put little glittery stickers of bugs and birds and flowers all over the box and label it with letter stickers:

MORGAN'S BOX OF WORDS!

I want to make him a giant box to root through, which we can point at things with or lay out in sequence on the floor to form sentences and phrases. It's hard not to think of the Houyhnhnms in *Gulliver's Travels*, who instead of using words carry around enormous sacks of objects that they can take out and point at.

I start by writing in marker on one of the cards: NURSE. Then, on the next: POPCORN. These are perhaps the two most frequent requests that Morgan makes in the course of a day and the two most contentious words in our vocabulary. He will not say them, no matter how badly he wants them. He will point my hand at the popcorn or grab Jennifer's hand and slap it against her breast, but he will not say the words.

Jennifer is in the middle of the living room, prompting him over and over: "Say it, Morgan. Say 'nurse.'"

He grabs Jennifer's hand and presses it more insistently against her chest.

"Morgan, nurse. Say 'nurse.'"

Jennifer turns to me. "Daddy, can you say 'nurse'?"

"Nurse!" I announce triumphantly.

"Good Daddy!"

"Mommy, can *you* say 'nurse'?"

"Nurse!" she says.

"Good Mommy!" I turn to Morgan. "Morgan, can *you* say 'nurse'?"

He walks away in disgust. He'd rather go hungry than talk.

So this is why these are our first two words on the cards.

"Are you going to use all capital letters?" Jennifer asks as I write.

"I guess. Does it matter?"

"Well, ninety percent of the letters in a sentence are lowercase."

I hadn't thought of that.

"Fair enough." I crumple up the cards and start rewriting them.

Morgan is spinning himself dizzy in the middle of the living room; he stumbles out of it and comes over to watch me write. He wants the marker; he wants the stack of blank cards; he wants the card that I am in the middle of writing.

"Hang on, sweetie." I push his hand away. "Okay, here you go."

popcorn

He eyes this dubiously, then watches as I write the next card. After about a dozen cards, he finally stops trying to grab them from me as I write, and instead grabs them the moment I lift up the marker. He is arranging them in a deck. In fact, he began arranging them as soon as there were two of them, looking over both carefully and determining: this goes on top, that goes on the bottom. The process repeats with each new card. This goes on until I have filled out a few hundred cards and stop out of sheer fatigue, though I know there are hundreds more words that he knows by sight.

Morgan curls against Jennifer, his hands barely fitting around the fat Day-Glo stack of cards, peering intently at each and then shuffling it to the bottom. He does this over, and over, and then over again, in intense silence. Jennifer begins to doze off; she cannot move because he is cozied up to her.

"You want me to take over furniture duty?"

"If you can."

I try to ease Morgan forward a little so that Jennifer can slip away and I can take her place, but he bats his hands around at me.

"Okay, okay." I turn to her. "Looks like you're stuck."

Eventually we do manage to change over, and I sit and watch him. He reads a card, then holds it over the next card as a shield, revealing the letters of the new word one by one, before finally shuffling the old one to the bottom of the deck. I've seen him read books this way, too, slowly folding a page over to reveal each vertical row of letters. Cards and books are not words or sentences: they are endless chains of letters, a running ligature of code.

He keeps doing this, without a break. For *two hours*. I scarcely know of any adults who can stare at index cards for two unbroken hours, never mind three-year-olds. Just as I am about to give up—or, at least, to write off to permanent paralysis my arm that he has been leaning on—he breaks his hours of silence.

"T-o-o-t-h-p-a-s-t-e. *Too-paste*."

"Morgan! That's gr—"

"C-l-o-u-d. *Cloud*."

And I watch, stunned at first, then cheering him on, as he reads every card—hundreds of them—out loud. He does not look up at me at any point or smile, but he is clearly reading them for my benefit. *I can do this*.

It is getting late, past ten. When I take him to the bathroom to brush his teeth, he is still holding a neon green card. And when I set him down to nurse and go to sleep, he is still clutching it, holding it against his mother's breast and staring at the letters as he suckles. His eyes begin to close and then flutter open.

"S-h-a-d-o-w. *Shadow*."

He leaps out of bed and runs around the house repeating the word and looking for the rest of his cards. He finds them, squeals with delight, and then:

He is asleep.

CHAPTER 7

Sally and Anne have a box and a basket in front them. Sally puts a marble in the basket. Then she leaves the room. While Sally is gone, Anne takes the marble out of the basket and puts it in the box. When Sally comes back in, where will she look for her marble?

It's an easy question to answer: Sally will look in the basket, because she doesn't know yet that the marble has been moved. A typical three-year-old can figure it out, and indeed, in test after test they do figure it out. So, for that matter, can three-year-olds with Down's syndrome. It's not a hard question. Only . . . the autistic kids keep missing it. "Sally looks in the box," they will answer—if, of course, you get them to answer at all.

The Sally-Anne test is the classic demonstration of autism's defining characteristic: the lack of a *theory of mind*. Most autistic children do not distinguish between their own minds and other people's, and the notion that someone else might be thinking different thoughts or seeing things differently does not occur to them. They cannot imagine that Sally does not know what they themselves know. Nor will they follow another person's gaze or pointing fingers; if the other person could not be thinking or seeing anything different from themselves, there is no point.

Perhaps the most succinct expression of this dilemma comes quite inadvertently from a physicist. Wolfgang Pauli used to deride colleagues in theoretical physics who disagreed with him as "not even wrong." He meant this as a put-down—that the questions they were asking were so off-base that their answers were irrelevant. Yet Pauli's notion could also be applied to those who are autistic. They do not respond in expected ways to questions or to social cues . . . but then, only a person working from the same shared set of expectations could give a truly wrong answer. The autist is working on a different problem with a different set of parameters; they are not even wrong. For while we live in a world of *you* and *I*, the autistic child lives in a world of *I*. When an autistic child's speech is transcribed, entire classes of verbs may be missing from the child's vocabulary— specifically, terms that attribute a mental state to another person. *Believe*, or *think*, or *know* . . . all vanish. The concepts do not exist.

"He knew what a dodecahedron was, but he did not seem to know the meaning of such common words as *think* or *guess*," one child's case study noted.

And when a child cannot understand that another person has motives different from their own, another concept disappears: deception. They cannot see it, even when it is right in front of them.

After Bruno Bettelheim's suicide in 1990, respectful obituaries duly appeared in the newspapers. The *Times* was fairly typical; titled BRUNO BETTELHEIM DIES AT 86; PSYCHOANALYST OF VAST IMPACT, it noted that "Bettelheim was one of the few members of his profession to achieve international prominence." Two weeks later, the paper ran a heartwarming appreciation under the title REMEMBERING BRUNO BETTELHEIM, A FRIEND TO CHILDREN AND A CHAMPION OF LEARNING. But not everyone, it soon emerged, was so enamored of the saintly doctor. By November, the paper's headlines were reading

ACCUSATIONS OF ABUSE HAUNT THE LEGACY OF DR. BRUNO BET-
TELHEIM, and a letter from a former patient was starkly headlined
BETTELHEIM BECAME THE VERY EVIL HE LOATHED.

"He was a megalomaniac," the patient wrote, and his wards
"were a replica of the Nazi milieu Bettelheim supposedly loathed."

The trickle of doubters became a torrent, one that swept away
the doctor's life and work with shocking speed. Other former
patients wrote of abuse, and heartbroken staff ended years of
silence about his sham science. Bettelheim's books were found to be
plagiarized, his data fudged. It emerged that the elusive "doctor"
had no degree at all, with the sum of his training consisting of three
psych courses. And rather than a protégé handpicked by Freud,
Bettelheim had been something rather more prosaic in Vienna: a
lumber salesman. His charisma had deterred anyone from checking his references, and in time his faked Viennese reputation was
supplanted by a real American one so immense that nobody
dreamed of questioning it.

But by the time he died, Bettelheim's theories were already
becoming disregarded within the profession. Indeed, things were
coming full circle. Even as Bettelheim's body was laid to rest, a
curiously familiar voice was about to reemerge from the dead. In
1991, Uta Frith, one of the researchers behind the Sally-Anne study,
brought the forgotten German thesis of Hans Asperger back to life
in an English translation. Bettelheim and Kanner had never referred
to their fellow alum in their writings, and it was only with the
belated translation of Asperger that many English speakers began to
understand that autism included a whole spectrum of permanent
outsiders, some so well adapted that they scarcely realized they had
been autistic all along. Rather than helpless primal casualties,
Asperger insisted, autists were talented eccentrics living among

us, albeit in a sphere of their own. A number were brilliant; many were also solitary and friendless. But Asperger had watched in amazement as some of his early cases flowered into mathematicians, engineers, chemists, and musicians—they were, he marveled, "usually in highly specialized academic professions, often in very high positions, with a preference for abstract content."

The boy with "grossly autistic behavior" who had been calculating cubic roots in preschool? As a young student, he discovered a mathematical error in one of Newton's calculations. He went on to become a professor of astronomy.

What he and other autists had was a single-mindedness that matched them perfectly with their work: indeed, some lived for little else. Wherever they were learning these skills, though, it was not at school. Teachers judged them rebellious or idiotic or both, and testing was of little help, either: a child who will not register a direct command will hardly give a response to an exam question. One boy, Asperger recalled, would flee from the cruelties of his school by hiding in a watchmaker's shop next to the school gates. The watchmaker, his shop a collection of minute mechanical intricacies, befriended the boy over philosophical conversations. Perhaps he recognized in the boy someone much like himself. But if this cognitive underground existed quietly throughout society, where was it coming from?

I caught one glimpse back in Britain: it was through an old oak door.

"You go across the courtyard," the elderly porter points. "In that building, through the door in the back, and to your left on Nevile Court."

"All right."

"Not right. Left. You go left."

"All . . . yes. Left." I back quickly out of the porter's office. "I'll go left."

I stroll out into the quadrangle and keep off the well-tended lawn. The medieval buildings loom up on every side and box you into insignificance. Trinity College is such an ancient part of Cambridge University that the first people who marveled at its ancient history are now themselves ancient history. You wonder how anyone gets any thinking done here, when the overriding thought as you sit at a desk must be: What an old piece of wood this is!

I enter a monumental stone building and stroll about looking for the door the porter mentioned. I don't see it. Or—no, that can't be it. Can it? Set into the back wall is a very small door that appears to have been retrieved from J. R. R. Tolkien's garage sale. It is perhaps five feet high and studded all over with dungeonlike bits of massy hand-hammered iron. Surely this is not the door I was directed to. Yet I do not see any other here.

I look around: I am alone. It is like some sort of senseless dream. I find the heavy iron handle, turn it, and duck my head down. I emerge crouching, half expecting to walk through some ridiculous magical portal into a jousting match. But no, there is only another quadrangle, looking just like the last. I do not see any other people— does anyone actually attend this institution?—and when I find the stairwell to Dr. Simon Baron-Cohen's office, each stair on the way up groans like a distinctly different human voice. I have been imbibing his neurological treatises on the flight over; they have been gushing out of this quiet building in the two decades since he helped create the Sally-Anne test.

I knock: nothing. There is no light on. I check my watch, sit by the window across the hallway. The dead stillness of the building is such that I can hear my ears ringing with disuse. I stare out of the casement window onto the quadrangle and look in vain once again for students. It was these students who provided Baron-Cohen, in the years after he worked with Uta Frith in the original Sally-Anne study, with some curious clues about the origins of autism.

This question has haunted autism research from the very beginning. Bettelheim, of course, blamed the parents. Asperger's gaze also fell upon the family, though from a different angle. Lost in a long silence after the Allied bombing of Vienna was a remarkable observation made near the end of Asperger's 1943 thesis, one whose import was not fully recognized for decades: "We have been able to discern related incipient traits in the parents or relatives," he wrote, "in *every* single case . . ." So if shadowy precursors of autism can be seen in an autist's family—if it shapes their very minds and talents— what might you expect to find? Perhaps men whose solitary pursuits, deep focus, and fascination with logical systems was matched only by their social awkwardness?

"The paradigm occupation for such a cognitive profile," Dr. Baron-Cohen has theorized, "is engineering."

When one thousand British parents of autistic children were then surveyed, the children proved to have fathers working in engineering at double the national rate. Science and accounting—solitary professions requiring deep focus and abstraction—showed even higher multiples in autistic families, and artists were represented at nearly quadruple the normal rate. When Baron-Cohen and other researchers narrowed their focus to the highest echelon of academic talent—that is, to students here at Cambridge—science majors had autism in their families at *six times* the rate of literature students.

Baron-Cohen's results led some to dub autism "geek syndrome." Computer programming is our most famously geeky profession; but when you remember that programming is merely a subset of mathematics, you realize why math departments are jokingly referred to as a jobs program for autists. Math is pure geekdom: its own universe, the absolute expression of abstract logic. One of Baron-Cohen's most striking case studies is of DB, a brilliant mathematician with two other mathematician brothers. A fourth brother is a low-functioning autist; their father is a physics lecturer. DB seems to be fairly socially successful, since he did manage to get married . . . to another mathematician. Yet DB was so oblivious of basic social interactions that "until he was told it was odd, he would run everywhere—down corridors, streets, etc., even if he was not in a hurry, just because it seemed efficient."

Some autists express great fondness for *Star Trek*'s Mr. Spock, whose plight mirrors their own: the logician from another world, baffled by our own. But such otherworldly eccentrics have always been a constant in math, right alongside the value of pi. One nineteenth-century comic lithograph, *Mathematical Abstraction*, shows an absentminded professor seated between his breakfast table and fireplace, gazing intently at an egg in his hand, while his watch boils in a saucepan. It was only a slight exaggeration of the greatest British math prodigy, Sir William Rowan Hamilton, who worked in a dining room covered in snowdrifts of his notes, barely interrupting himself to eat when his family brought him a pork chop. After his death in 1865, the dining room was opened and, one colleague reported, "the literary remains were wheeled out and examined, [and] china plates with the relics of food upon them were found between the sheets of manuscript, plates sufficient in number to furnish a kitchen."

But it was that obliviousness to the interruptions of the outside world, Hamilton once explained, that made his line of work possible:

"The only difference between an ordinary mind and the mind of Sir Isaac Newton consists principally in this—that the one is capable of a more continuous application than the other."

There is something endearing in such minds; I've always been partial to John Fransham, the eighteenth-century mathematician who as a teenager spent a £25 inheritance on a pony—"not to ride, but to make a friend of"—whereupon his physician concluded the young man was "out of his wits." Fransham invented a ball-and-cup game that he played incessantly until he'd caught the ball 666,666 times. He wrote on philosophy but could be thrown by the simplest activities; once, when writing a letter asking for money, he was utterly stymied by the fact that he'd never folded a piece of paper before. He never did send the letter.

Rain taps at the window next to my head, and I trace out geometric figures on my unused notepad. I'm still alone. I check my watch and start wondering when the next express train back to London is, when there is a clattering up the stairs, as if someone is tumbling *up* them, and a flustered woman appears.

"Paul Collins? Are you Paul Collins?"

"Yes?"

"You must come quickly," she says as we bustle down the staircase. "Professor Baron-Cohen is to meet you at his home."

There is a taxi waiting when we exit the quadrangle, and it whisks us through the city and down rows of pleasant residences; I am disgorged into a yard filled with brightly colored plastic toys. For a strange moment, it looks like *my* yard. But the house I am led into is unfamiliar; the assistant vanishes, and now I am staring at the polished cross section of a tree on a wall and jars of dried beans arranged on a shelf by Baron-Cohen's breakfast table.

"Do you take sugar in your tea?" he asks from the kitchen.

I look at the house around me, still a little bewildered. "One would be great, thanks."

"I'm sorry I couldn't reach you earlier. My son's not feeling well, and so . . ." He wordlessly indicates his parental house arrest.

"Oh, it's quite all right. I have a three-year-old son . . . I know how it is."

"Ah. So you do know."

Baron-Cohen must have been quite a youngster himself, certainly no more than a grad student, when the famous marbles and baskets were first brought out. Despite bursting into the field with the Sally-Anne test nearly twenty years ago, he is still tousled and bright. I watch as he stirs the milk into the tea and brings the cups over to the table.

"So," I ask, "I was curious about your studies linking engineering and math . . ."

"We've been looking to extend the engineering study into the tendency toward *systemizing* among the autistic and their families," he says as he sits down. "This encompasses a range of activities, as well as professions like engineering." It means file clerks and accountants. It means puzzle fanatics and musicians. It means the autistic prodigy in theoretical physics, who patiently explained to Baron-Cohen and his team that "my mind is like a digital computer: it is either on or off. Information is either true or false. Other people's minds are like analog computers, with smoothly varying voltages, and manifesting fuzzy logic." And it means that boy's father, a plane spotter who can list the entire contents of his own enormous record collection . . . as well as the lyrics.

We hear people at the door.

"That must be them," he says suddenly. "I'm afraid I'm rather having to juggle appointments today. I'll introduce you."

Two women walk in: a television producer and Dr. Fiona Scott, who is leading a large survey of autism among British schoolchildren.

"It's early days yet," Baron-Cohen explains to me as they join us at the table, "but we're working on a documentary on autism."

"That part we are certain of." The producer smiles at me. "As for everything else . . ."

The conversation goes back and forth as they try to shape the documentary. Do they show just autistic children? What about autistic teenagers? Adults? Old people? Do they focus on the gee-whiz savants and successes? What about the low-functioning, the retarded, the emotionally troubled, and the suicidal autists? What about the profoundly autistic, rocking back and forth and flapping their hands, eternally short-circuited from human contact? But what if that makes the parents despair over their children? And how about . . .

Where does one even start?

"I think"—Dr. Scott folds her hands together—"lack of diagnosis is an important issue. Profound autism won't go undiagnosed. But others along the spectrum do."

"Hmm."

"We've been finding a significant discrepancy between diagnosed rates of autism and actual rates," she turns to me to explain. "And this is in Cambridgeshire. This is how much they're missing here, in *Cambridgeshire*. In the more remote districts, well . . ."

Her point hangs in the air.

"So the early detection is worth emphasizing." The producer jots in her notebook.

Baron-Cohen nods thoughtfully.

"There is one constant refrain we hear from people diagnosed with autism in adulthood." He leans forward. "They might feel it changes nothing to know now. But they always say this to us: 'I wish had known when I was young.'"

The producer and I dash down the platform for the train to Waterloo Station.

"A close one there." She smiles across the aisle as doors are banged shut on each train car. Then we both set about scribbling notes in our respective notepads, with her dashing down ideas for the TV show, and me . . . well, actually, I just sort of stare at my sheet. Then I slowly, idly, tear a page out, spiral by spiral.

Click *click* click *click*: we are slowly picking speed, and a man sitting next to me is tapping away at his laptop, working in time with the trestles. I look around. Here we are, a crowded rush-hour train full of people, drinking from little Volvic bottles as we hurtle along the track, talking into cell phones and playing Minesweeper on computers, and yet . . . how many of us know *how* we're doing it? We know *what* to do: we read the electronic signs at the station, we get on the train being dragged by a massive diesel motor, we sit down and talk via satellites. But who on earth understands how the computerized station sign—or this train engine—or this phone—or the satellite—or the machine that wove the pattern into my seat's cushion—how do these things work? What kind of people even get this stuff? I am clothed and fed and moved by processes that are absurdly complicated and that I live completely oblivious to. We are one of the first generations to operate in almost total ignorance about the creation of every single physical object that we encounter in the course of a day. We are hapless generalists stranded in a specialist world, and we just muddle through because it's best that way, it's easiest.

I glance across the aisle: The producer is still taking notes on her television show. And did you know?—I don't understand how the hell TVs work, either.

I look down at the piece of paper torn out of my notepad, which I have been unconsciously folding and unfolding. I draw a pen out of my coat and quietly list out the occupations of Morgan's immediate male relatives, plus his parents. Science, art, and math: the autism trifecta. Apparently we have been walking around with the genetic equivalent of a KICK ME sign:

my father: mechanical engineer
jennifer's father: musician, math major
my brother: phd in computing
jennifer: painter

me

CHAPTER 8

I was ordered to see the nurse or the principal just about every day of 1974. I was a discipline problem; I'd bolt from the kindergarten classroom and clap my hands over my ears to shut it all out, and I'd bite anyone who tried to drag me back. They found this worrisome. And when they did get me back into the classroom, I wouldn't respond to their questions, didn't even seem to hear them. That, they decided, was even more worrisome.

I liked the nurse's office; unlike the principal, she kept her blinds open. Through the windows you could see the front lawn, the flagpole, and the school's sign: NEW HANOVER UPPER FREDERICK ELEMENTARY SCHOOL. The sunlight came in on metal cabinets that were cool to the touch, linoleum floors the color of chocolate milk, and my own favorite, a huge ancient glass jar filled with cotton balls. It was quiet in her office; I liked that. It meant that I was away from my teacher and from the other kids.

The nurse stood by as the audiologist fitted the chunky headphones around my head. "Paul," she said, her voice distant through the beige plastic, "I want you to raise your hand when you hear a sound in there. Okay?"

I nodded.

Then I waited.

eeeeeeEEEEEEeeeeeeee

I raised my hand.

The cards are arranged across Morgan's bedroom floor, nonsensical but in ramrod straight formation:

sleepy dog popsicle drink

We find the index cards all over the house: under the cushions, stuffed between mattresses, wedged into heating vents. Yesterday I found one inside his diaper, jammed between his legs: **jump**, it commanded them. On the windowpane that overlooks our street I find **outside**, slid into the bottom corner like a curatorial note; a closet mirror in his bedroom is existentially labeled **you**.

But right now Morgan is sitting in Jennifer's lap, having a long conversation with a deck of alphabet flash cards. He is looking at a card with U on one side and a picture of a unicorn on the reverse.

"Hey-yo, Mayamaga," he says.

"Hey-yo, naya U," he replies to himself.

"Hey-yo, maga."

Then he flips over the card.

"Hey-yo, uncone."

"Uh-oh. Aya donna lie that."

I sit down and move Morgan to my lap so that Jennifer can stand up and stretch; Morgan has already been doing this for an hour straight with her.

"What do you think he's saying?" she asks.

Morgan picks another card out of the deck, without the slightest hint of being aware that he and his words are the object of intense scrutiny.

"I have no idea," I finally admit.

After a while, though, it begins to make sense. It is a conversation between Morgan and *a letter:*

> *The Letter U:* Hello, Mommy and Morgan.
>
> *M:* Hello, letter U.
>
> *U:* Hello, Morgan.
>
> M: Hello, unicorn. Uh-oh, I do not like that.

At which point he puts the card away. He is quoting a line from the book *Go Dog Go*. A female dog tries on different hats, asking, "Hello, do you like my hat?"—and the male invariably rejoinders with, "I do not like that hat." These lines are always Morgan's favorite part of the book. He has interpreted the phrase to mean "Now we will change to something new." So he says it before moving on to the next alphabet card. Our son is spending hours having animated conversations with letters of the alphabet, letters that greet him and say hello to him and his mother. And now that I'm holding him in my lap, the letters greet me, too: *"Hey-yo, Daya."*

I work with letters and words for a living, but I have never been greeted by one before.

My living is that of a historian, which means I sequence fragments and then extrapolate a world from them. I've done it every day of my life. It never occurred to me that I was different from anyone else; I thought everyone was this way. For one thing, my childhood hearing tests came out just fine. Better than fine, in fact: my hearing was almost preternaturally heightened. My school didn't know what to make of that. But the following year, I had a new teacher who was much nicer than the old one. And I remember making friends for the first time, too. I had been placed in special ed.

I have learned, over the years, to work around my selective hearing. Facing someone, one-on-one, in deep conversation, I hear everything. But otherwise, my attention wanders: It becomes fixed upon some other noise or activity in the room. More often, it will jump tracks to things internal and completely unrelated: I must remember to buy a new shower rod; I wonder why D'Israeli's work has not been reprinted; maybe he is not reliable enough in his sources; hey, what about those old Canadian Club ads where they'd go up and bury a case of whiskey on a glacier for you to find, and—

Blub bub bar guh blub **Paul.**

When more than a few seconds have elapsed between sentences, I am near deaf. Probably I can hear my name; that will get my attention, and I will then look up:

Blub bub bar guh blub **Paul.**

There are two possible outcomes to this sentence for me. First, I work backward, trying to remember each bit of what I unheard just before the "Paul." Sometimes there are bits of words caught in there, just enough to work with:

Cyc, cull, icicle, cycling, recycle, recycling:

recycling Paul

ow, ot, out

out recycling Paul

who, through, you

you out recycling Paul

At this point I can extrapolate:

Did you take out the recycling, Paul?

"No . . . Has the garbage truck already come by?"

Either my wife will give me a puzzled look and repeat a totally different but vaguely homonymic sentence—"Should we take Morgan out to the mall?"—or, if I have guessed right, our conversation will continue normally from there. But it always takes me a moment before I can deliver that first guesswork reply, which probably gives me a vaguely absent and distracted air.

A lot of the time I can't even guess what the words are. So several dozen times a day—sometimes between every other sentence in our more languorous living room conversations—Jennifer will hear:

"I'm sorry . . . What?"

But this is not the reason that my mom remembers.

"Well," she says over the phone, "you were not quite *mature* yet."

I lean against the frame of the kitchen doorway, cradling the phone in my shoulder, watching Morgan in the living room. He is pressing his face up against his computer screen, examining each pixel.

"You just weren't quite ready for a regular class," she explains over the phone. "You were immature. So they put you in a special class."

"Slow class."

"A special class."

"Special ed."

"Well . . ."

"It was special ed," I insist.

"It was just because you weren't . . . mature yet."

"Mom, I was six years old."

"Well . . . yes, but . . ." She is trying hard to be soothing. "You would have these *fits*."

"Fits?"

"With your feet. And your hands. It was when you got frustrated."

Oh. Those.

Nobody ever asked me *why* I stomped my feet, or screamed, or thrashed around with my arms. I probably couldn't have explained it anyway. It happened like that only at school. *I just wanted everyone to shut up.* It was overwhelming—horrible—the blast of noise of everyone talking at once, everyone singing at once, everyone looking at me at the same time when my turn came for something, and *why can't they stop it?* The radius of my flailing arms and legs formed a bubble in which I could enclose myself, like the clear plastic balls that hamsters roll around in.

It made me feel *calm*—in a frantic sort of way.

"I thought I was in that class because of my hearing."

"N-no . . ." My Mom hesitates. "It was the fits. What's wrong with your hearing?"

"They didn't tell you?"

"No."

"They kept testing me. They thought I was deaf. But I wasn't. It's just that I sort of focus . . . I don't know. I don't hear anything when I'm working. I just focus, and the hours go, and I don't hear anything. If someone tries to talk to me, it's like they're trying to shake me awake. It's exactly like that, actually."

There is a short, strange silence—and then I suddenly hear a broad guffaw. I've forgotten that my dad is on another extension, listening as he cooks in their kitchen.

"Oh, that's bloody marvelous," he sputters.

"What?"

My dad sets down a pot on his end. "You," he says, "have just described your mother."

"Oh, Jack . . ."

"Seriously?" I press, though I know he's right. I've seen it.

"Well, maybe you do get that part from me," my mom admits. "But your father is responsible for everything else."

Everything else. I envision my dad's drafting table and his drawing instruments; they were brushed metal, expensive, German. When I was a kid I'd watch him withdraw the mechanical pencils, the stencils, and the compass from their cases and set about blue-printing a chocolate-tempering line, a hard-candy enrober, an entire factory. I couldn't figure out how he kept it all in his head; I lived around machines of every variety, but how did a man design one? Lots of professions seemed unfathomably complicated to me when I was a kid. Some still do.

Bill Gates is staring at me and smiling in a rather unnerving way. I shift uneasily in my chair.

WHERE DO YOU WANT TO GO TODAY?

I don't know.

I finally break away from the gaze of the clumsily taped-up poster on the lobby wall of Microsoft HQ. Somehow I'd expected a hologram of the guy to greet me by name, or at least an animatronic Bill in the style of the Country Bear Jamboree. But no, it's just a torn poster. *Where do you want to go today?* I drum my fingers against the plastic of the chair. Where *did* I go today, exactly? They asked me up here to do a meet-the-author thing with their employees, but what I really want to do is meet their autism researchers. Outside I can see men and women strolling through the Microsoft plaza, talking into cell phones, lugging gym bags, tapping at pocket assistants. *Buzz buzz buzz.* I wonder how many wireless signals are passing through my body right now.

I've been able to shoehorn in a meeting with a researcher, Lili Cheng, before I have to give my author talk, and the conference room I am led to is all you'd expect: anonymous, the room temperature just right, the broadband access all in place, the video monitor at the ready, the chairs comfy. But we cannot keep the lights on.

"Microsoft's work actually started with Hutch World, which was an online community we developed for cancer patients," Lili says. "But for . . ."

The room goes dark, and she sighs heavily.

"I'll get it this time," I say.

I wave my hands around. Nothing. I stand up and raise my arms in supplication to the fluorescent bulbs: they grudgingly flicker back on.

"Those room motion detectors are really bad," she marvels. "Anyway, out of Hutch World we developed KidTalk."

"And that was with the Autism Center?"

"Right." She nods and sets up the video monitor. "It's where we're developing and testing it."

Which seems appropriate; one of Bill Gates's biographers has raised the possibility that the man may have Asperger's Syndrome. This was met with a deafening official silence from Redmond. But now there's a new Autism Center at the University of Washington, just across the bridge from the software giant—founded with a multimillion-dollar grant from "an unnamed Microsoft executive."

Lili unveils the project on the monitor. "Okay, here it is . . . it's quite different from Hutch World."

I watch the KidTalk program unfold on the screen. Some autistic kids won't talk; others can't stop lecturing you on dinosaurs, or trains, or stars, or the fine points of refrigeration technology. But they can't tell when they're talking inappropriately; they can't read the signals. Nobody is keeping score of the conversation for them. And that, in effect, is what KidTalk does.

On one side is the thread of ongoing conversations being typed in by autistic kids talking with, between, and mostly past one another. On the other side, each autist has his or her own kid-shaped icon, resembling a cutout animation from *South Park*. A moderator moves it around during the conversation; if a kid talks too much, the icon moves to the center and its mouth gapes comically wide; if the child doesn't talk enough, the icon drifts to the periphery of the screen and slumps its head back to fall asleep. If you get it just right—if you can fake your way through a normal human conversation—then you circulate comfortably among the other participants, your icon bearing a happy face.

"It's still in the pilot stage," Lili says. "But we've been working on it and developing it with the . . . Autism . . . Center . . ."

She stops, and we both wave our arms in the air again, trying to get the lights back on.

*   *   *

I give my author lecture in another meeting room down the hall. This time the lights are staying on. But from the moment I begin talking, I see guys in the audience looking down. And then I hear it:

click. click. click-click.

They are staring deeply into laptops, tapping away.

At the end of the lecture, I drain out from the meeting room along with the crowd, reminding myself to talk to one of the participants when we meet for dinner downtown. On the cab ride over, I watch the Redmond campus recede behind me and think about the man behind it all: Alan Turing.

Turing was the enigmatic young Cambridge mathematical logician who laid the foundations of modern digital computing; unlike predecessors who envisioned single-purpose mechanical adding machines, in 1936 Turing imagined a *universal* machine that used binary logic to perform any number of different tasks. Only his paper wasn't about machines: there were no such computers for nearly another decade. "Computers" meant *people who compute*; Turing thought he'd unraveled the workings of the human brain. Mental operations were, at some fundamental level, analogous to a sort of series of numerical routines and subroutines.

Turing went on to quietly save the world. Holed up in the supersecret cryptography lab at Bletchley Park during World War II, he developed theories that helped crack the German Enigma machine and created one of the first modern computers to handle the decoding. Turing is held up today as the founder of artificial intelligence, but he'd have removed the word *artificial*; he had found the key not just to thinking machines, but to all thinking. Hence his famous "Turing test": when a digital computer could converse believably enough to fool a human being, it was fully intelligent. There was nothing artificial about it.

But his test relied on communication through a "teleprinter," so that pesky data like physical gestures could be ignored; the test doesn't show you how humans think any better than dogs walking on their hind legs show you how people walk. When a computer tries to crunch words, meaning gets pulverized. Going into a canned routine whenever the logic of a certain string or frequency of words dictates it can go woefully wrong, because human language is not always . . . well, *logical*. You can flummox just about any such program with irony, double meaning, or cultural references—lyrics, book or band titles, tag lines from TV shows—that in themselves make no literal sense. Turing tried, but it's damnably difficult to resolve human life into logical Boolean statements.

That Turing even thought computers were like humans is the curious thing—but then, Turing was a curious fellow. He had always focused intensely on science, could barely be bothered with learning communication in school, and was strangely naïve about reading the intentions of others; his attention was far away, his eyes unable to focus on people when they spoke; his body was clumsy, and his brain was rigorous. In 1936 no one yet could name or conceptualize what might have forged Turing's strange demeanor. That was still years away, awaiting a little-noticed physician in a Viennese pediatric clinic.

"Okay . . ." I lean toward the employee as we're waiting for our food. "Here's what I can't figure out about Microsoft."

"This should be good."

"No, it's just a little thing. It was when I was talking to the audience. There were guys typing into laptops right from the beginning, when I was just saying hi. Before I even opened my *mouth*. I mean, what could they be possibly taking notes on?"

"They weren't taking notes," she says.

"What do you mean?"

"They were watching the company's internal webcast of your talk."

I puzzle over this as the plates arrive.

"They were sitting *twenty feet away* from me."

"Doesn't matter. That's how they prefer to watch people."

"Why?"

She sets her fork down.

"Listen, they're different. They actually have someone there full-time, and all she does is try to take these programmers on field trips. Those guys live at Microsoft. *That's all they do.* They go to the campus to work, they sleep in their apartment on the edge of campus, they wake up and go back into the campus again. They *won't* do anything else. They don't *know* what else to do. So that's this woman's whole job. She books places just so that the programmers and math theorists get a night out."

"That would be interesting to see."

"Hmph. I think one time they booked the symphony, just for Microsoft, so the musicians were playing to all these programmers. Only these guys in the audience had all their phones and their gadgets with them, and they wouldn't stop using them during the performance . . . and, well, they were sort of not asked back."

"Understandably."

"But see, the programmers didn't *know*. Seriously. They really didn't know that they weren't supposed to do that . . ." She searches for the words. "It's . . . it's as if they have to be taught how to act around actual human beings. Because they just don't know."

Really, how does anyone know? Imagine if you tried to pretend to understand people, but didn't really. So you rehearse it all in your head: taking notes, analyzing every social action, trying to connect it all together. And if you just hit upon the right formulas, the right set of actions, the right buzzwords, you would have it down—*you could fit in*. Imagine your entire life as an endless Turing test.

When will they figure out that you're not one of them?

PART THREE

DEAR CHROMOPHONE

CHAPTER 9

His little hand grasps mine as we follow a maze of signs and arrows down the long linoleum hall: BARB'S CLASSROOM THIS WAY, they read. We have to stop at each sign so that he can grab my index finger and jam it against the words like a lecturer's pointer.

"Barb's . . . classroom . . . this . . . way . . ."

He moves my finger back.

"Classroom," I repeat. Jab. Jab. Jab. "Classroom. Classroom. Morgan, *ouch*. Gentle with Daddy."

We get to the last sign, posted on a door: BARB'S CLASSROOM.

"Classroom." My finger is getting rapped against the door like a cast-iron knocker. "Classroom. Classroom." The door opens and Morgan charges straight into the arms of the teacher.

"Morgan! I got Morgan! Morganmorganmorgan!" Barb tickles him as he collapses in giggles.

I look around Morgan's new classroom; we are the last to arrive today. Everyone else is already here. The sweet one who has panic attacks. The cute one who smiles but won't talk. The heart-breaking one with the strange skull who keeps crying and crying. And me and my son. Each one has a teacher or an assistant at his or her side.

"Okay . . ." Barb lolls Morgan back, burbling with laughter at the ceiling, then stands him up straight. "Let's see what's on your schedule."

He follows her, still dazed from giggling, over to four Velcro strips on the wall, each with a relabeled old yogurt cup attached: they read MORGAN, DYLAN, KWAME, and NATHANIEL. A line of cards, each bearing an icon and a phrase, is Velcro taped in a stripe next to each cup:

TABLE TIME

BALL PIT

MOTOR ROOM

SNACK

CIRCLE TIME

Morgan's cup is covered with a slotted lid. Barb places a red plastic chip in Morgan's hand and guides it to his cup; they drop in the chip. Then she hands him the TABLE TIME card. Every activity here has its visual sign; everything is broken down into repeatable routines.

Morgan tugs at his overall straps and looks with curiosity at the squeeze bottles of paint on a table. Dylan, the sweet-natured one of the group, is squealing happily as he dabs fingerpaint across a giant sheet of newsprint. "Do you want to paint?" Barb asks, and deftly drops a plastic smock over Morgan as she sits him down at a table. She pours out a pool of blue paint and guides Morgan's fingers into it. His face wrinkles a little in doubt; the paint is cold and wet and viscous.

"He likes brushes," I venture. Jennifer has pickle jars bristling with them in her studio, and Morgan will grab quiverfuls to stroke the soft bristles against his face, the floors, the walls, his clothes. So Barb digs through a box of art supplies and pulls out a little brush.

He promptly presses into the paint, smearing the brush back and forth, tapping it around, dappling the paper.

Out of the corner of my eye, I see Dylan's father quietly slip out of the room; he smiles and nods at me as he leaves. But he is a little apprehensive. The door clicks shut behind me and I hear him walk slowly, hesitantly, down the hallway. It takes only a few seconds.

Dylan looks up and around, and a look of profound soundless upset passes over his face. He curls over and begins to hyperventilate. Then he screams, *"Daddy-y-y-yyee."* He is inconsolable. A teacher presses his sides—the pressure calms them—she talks soothingly, she distracts him, and he will not stop crying.

"Daddy!" the boy gasps.

If you tell him his father is coming back soon, it makes no difference. He is not here right now. *He is not here.*

Morgan looks up briefly at the commotion. Then, unruffled, he keeps painting.

Back and forth: forth and back.

"Hi," the little girl says as he runs past.

It's our first day off from school, and we're at the park a couple of blocks from our house. Morgan runs onward to the playground trash can and carefully—painstakingly—drops a wood chip into it. Then he runs back again and grabs another piece of landscaping bark off the ground; he examines it minutely and then wordlessly hurries it over to the trash can on his endless project. We nearly have the playground to ourselves—just me, him, and a little girl whose mother is resting on a rickety bench.

The girl pulls her arms inside her puffy pink jacket and hops up and down.

"Hi," she says again.

Morgan rushes past.

I look to the mother with a helpless shrug, and she shrugs, too.

"Hi!" I smile to the girl.

The girl waves back silently and skips away.

Morgan runs up a play structure, making his happy noise—*dukka dukka dukka*—and flapping his hands; then he rappels steadily up the rubber climbing disks, his strong little arms pulling hard. When he reaches the top he looks up at the sky, blinking and wordless.

Clop clop clop: The little girl runs up the gangway, too.

"Hi," she yells up to him.

Morgan is looking at the sky.

"Hi. Hi-iii," she repeats.

Morgan's eyes shift, but he does not look at her.

"Hi!" I cut in. "How are you?"

"I'm okay." She dances back down the gangway and to her mother. Morgan does not watch them leave.

"Morgan, when someone says 'Hi' to you, you say 'Hi' back."

Nothing.

"Cold." He presses his cheek against the jungle gym. "Cold."

"That's right." I run my hand over the metal. "Cold. Br-r-r!"

He slaps the hollow metal pipe, letting it ring out into the silence. *Bing*. He does it again and then again. Then he moves to the next pipe and slaps that one, too. *Kong*.

They are not quite the same length: they hold slightly different notes. He leans into it, staring deeply.

Kong.

He moves back to the first pipe, hits that—then to the second pipe again. *Kong*. He regards the two pipes together, then separately, as the ghostly reverberation lingers, his face blank in thought. Then he stares into the distance across the Sunnyside playground. We have the place to ourselves now; there is nothing else to interrupt the weekend silence of the local schoolyard, the abandoned calm of an old brick building and fading playground macadam, the silent swaying of the basketball nets in the wind.

"Co-o-o-ld," he repeats.

"Check this out." Marc nods down at Morgan. "He's been doing this ever since I started my shift with him this afternoon."

I sit on the edge of Morgan's bed and watch. He pulls out a foam rubber letter from an alphabetical set in one corner of his bedroom, then walks over to his Talking Big Bird doll in the other corner and presses it into the doll's plastic hand.

"E," he explains to the mute bird.

He bats the letter against the doll's hand a few times, then takes it back to the other side of the room. Then he comes back again with another.

"F." Bat, bat.

He continues on, oblivious to our watching him.

"He was doing this outside yesterday, too," Marc says. "You know those little lava rocks that they have in their garden next door?"

"Mmm-hmm."

"He was picking them up and bringing them over to Big Bird, and showing them to him."

Big Bird stares ahead: expressionless, motionless.

"G," Morgan tells him, then takes the letter away.

"He doesn't show stuff to kids at the playground."

"They're too hyper. They want to *talk*."

We watch him in silence as he goes through more letters. But upon reaching P, Morgan stops. He wordlessly grabs Marc and

117

pushes him through the doorway and toward the kitchen, like moving a checker piece from one square to the next. Then he holds Marc's hand and points it up at the shelf.

"Popcorn? You want popcorn? Can you say the word?"

No.

"Popcorn? You want popcorn? Can you say it?"

No.

When we get to school a couple of days later, Morgan starts whimpering.

"It's okay. It's okay, honey. We're not going to class today."

The conference room inside is overheated, like every other room in this building. Morgan squirms uncomfortably between Jennifer and me.

"I think I have something to occupy him." Barb reaches into her teacher's bag and pulls out a deck of cards: *Things That Go*. Fighter jet, forklift, dump truck, fishing boat . . . Morgan studies each with deep and endless seriousness and then draws my finger to them for me to pronounce them. After each one he pronounces it as well, in his own way, then moves carefully to the next card.

"Helicopter," I say.

"A-hey-ya-coppa-coppa."

"Does he often add syllables like that?" Barb asks.

"Yeah, he does."

"Purple rectango-ango."

Morgan is running a finger around the shape of one of his cards. There is no purple anywhere on the card, and I notice Barb looking at him curiously.

"It's his Talking Big Bird doll," I explain. "It has plastic blocks that you put in its hand, and it identifies their shape and color. So he's just started identifying all squares as orange squares, and rectangles as purple rectangles . . . that kind of thing."

Morgan glances up for the briefest moment at Barb's stare, then looks backs into his cards.

"Well," she says. "That *is* interesting."

I shrug and smile. I'm not worried. Everyone figures out eventually that purple is purple and rectangles are rectangles.

Bruce rolls in on his wheelchair. "Should we get started?"

"Sure. Okay, we wanted to go over some ideas with you for Morgan. He had a bit of a . . . a . . . ."

"Meltdown."

"Well, yes. A bit of a meltdown yesterday in class. He tried to bite the occupational therapist. Does he bite much at home?"

"Oh no, no, No. Sometimes."

I look down at Morgan, curled up against me with his cards, and I stroke his hair.

"Not when he's left alone," Jennifer muses.

"But? . . ."

"He's not aggressive. He is defensive, though. When he's working on something that he's focused on, he doesn't really care who is in the room. He only gets mad or notices them when they interrupt him."

"So transitioning between activities is a problem."

"It is. But he only really gets anxious . . . well, *here*. And we don't want him to hate school."

"I wonder," Bruce breaks in, "if we're moving him too fast into nonvisual work."

"I had that thought," Barb nods and turns to us. "Have you used PECS at home yet?"

"What's that?"

"Picture Exchange Communication System. It's what we're starting in the classroom. Morgan stares at symbols and reads, but he won't listen or converse. So we use that visual bias, his fixation on cards, as a toehold into communication. Everything has a card assigned to it. When he wants things, he uses the appropriate card. We move him up in small steps . . ."

She takes Jennifer's hand to demonstrate.

"First, you hold Morgan's hand, like I'm doing here, and work him through the motions of giving the card to Paul. Then, once he's used to that, he has to hand the card himself. Then he has to open your closed palm and hand you the card. Then he has to repeat what's written on the card. Then he has to say it on his own, without your cue. And then, eventually . . ."

She spreads her hands apart.

"Eventually, there's no card. Just words."

I stare down at him as he guides my finger across a *Things That Go* card.

"*Go-cart*. Well, we'd like to give that a try."

"Go-a-car."

"Good," Barb says. "So I need to make that first card for him. I can run it off on the computer right now. It needs to be something he's really motivated to ask for. Can you think of something like that?"

Jennifer and I look at each other.

"Yes," I answer. "We can."

I hold the thin laminated card in my hand.

"Popcorn. You said, '*I want popcorn.*' "

He has not actually said anything: but he is thinking it, and that is the first step. I hand Morgan a few pieces, and he puts them in his mouth, staring alternately at me and the bowl as he eats the popcorn. I put the card back on his desk and wait.

"Do you want more popcorn?" Jennifer asks. She is sitting behind him, her arms draped around him. He picks up the card, and Jennifer guides the card in his hand over to my outstretched palm. POPCORN, it reads, below a little colored icon of an old-fashioned movie popcorn box. I clasp my fingers around the card and give him a few more kernels out of the bowl in my lap.

"Good job! You said, '*I want popcorn.*'"

On it goes like this: for minutes, for hours, for weeks. Three of us, in a room, passing a single card back and forth, and the faint sound of a little boy crunching on popcorn.

CHAPTER 10

"Where can I find an account of a shipwreck, it is believed on an English ship, in which the crew lived for three days on a cask of raspberry jam?"

Before the Internet, there was *Notes and Queries*. It is the most perfect magazine of the Victorian era: a London weekly comprising bizarre questions to other readers and their even more bizarre answers. The raspberry jam query was typical, and you never knew who else would write in: a retired naval officer, say, with his jolly reminiscences on how *his* shipwrecked crew kept their starving stomachs full by swallowing lead shot. There are articles on a Bulgarian's obsession with the ethnographic distribution of fish hooks in America, and ancient clippings tracing the origin of the phrase *bull in a china shop*—an actual bull charged into the china shop of a Miss Powell on March 17, 1773, "where he frightened the lady into a hysterical fit"—and, naturally, broke her plates.

Many queries poked into arcane areas of science. One included this description of an Australian caterpillar: "Every one has a very curious plant, belonging to the fungi tribe, growing from the *anus*; this fungus varies from three to six inches in length, and bears at its extremity a blossom-like appendage, and evidently derives its nourishment from the body of the insect." Other queries are a little less earthy: "Have any works ever been published on the analogy between colours and musical sounds?" reads one in the June 21, 1862, issue. This letter is signed under a single, mysterious pseudonym: *Chromophone*.

There was indeed a book out there for Chromophone.

"So precise is the parallel of chromatics and music," argued color theorist George Field in 1817, "that whatever may be argued of the one may be asserted of the both." Field had already applied his very considerable talents in botany, chemistry, and optics to the service of the nation's artists: he'd developed a dazzling array of new lenses, cultivated plants for exotic new paint pigments, and exerted a powerful influence on his friend Henry Newton, the founder of the Winsor & Newton paint dynasty. Field also invented a process used to refine sugar, as well as designing stoves and similar contrivances.

But his true life's work remained his musical color theory. While it found favor among Pre-Raphaelite painters, it is virtually unknown today. His name is scarcely recognized even in the village where he was born in 1777—where, as a young child, he could see that town's most famous resident shambling through the streets, an aged but wild and silent enigma. And in this town, a few years later, he might pass Peter the Wild Boy's gravestone on a Sunday as he left church. Yet the two might have had much more in common than anyone, until quite recently, could ever have guessed.

Field is now as unknown as Peter himself. But among antiquarians, scuffed-up copies of *Chromatics: Or, The Analogy, Harmony, and Philosophy of Colours* change hands for thousands of dollars, for

Chromatics is itself a work of art. To illustrate his color keys and scales, Field and engraver David Lucas created fantastic plates worthy of Blake, showing the color-music scales superimposed against roiling clouds, storm-tossed seas, a fiery sunset. Our senses and all they took in, he argued, were intimately connected and moved in parallel. The scales are hand tinted in each copy, and page after page of their analogies grow and flourish wildly: from musical scales and colors to solids, curves, gradations of light and dark, to floral forms, to the human body itself.

Chromatics mushroomed into an even rarer work, *Outlines of Analogical Philosophy*—which, Field's subtitle promised, would weld together "Science, Nature, and Art." But the message of the illustrations in *Chromatics* was already unmistakable: the world itself is saturated with analogies among the senses, and it only remains for us to discover their governing laws.

The reply to Chromophone came in the July 12 issue of *Notes and Queries*:

> At the Soiree of the Musical Society of London, held at St. James's Hall last year, I exhibited a series of odorous bodies arranged to a scale of six octaves, each odour bearing its corresponding musical note. Many eminent musical savants there discussed the subject, and admitted that I had at least established my theory. To show facts, however, will require a series of difficult and recondite experiments. These I am pursuing. Will CHROMOPHONE help me solve the problem, the first problem of which I have laid down?
> G. W. Septimus Piesse.
> Chiswick.

It is a remarkable reply. Though scarcely anyone knows of Piesse today, in 1862 he was literally a household name—the brand on a million labels. It was as if Chromophone's letter had been answered by Betty Crocker. Yet I can't find a picture of Piesse even in his own book.

"I have the first and I think the third editions of *Chemical Magic*," Ricky Jay e-mails me. "There was a trick involving the frontispiece. It showed an empty picture frame with instructions to make a portrait of the author appear. To do this, you would hold a lighted match under the page.

"Needless to say," he adds, "this leaf is not extant in all copies."

A perfect vanishing act to the last, Piesse's visage was scorched out of existence by his readers—just as his life's work vanished, molecule by volatile molecule, into the atmosphere. One magazine ad from 1864 reads:

PIESSE AND LUBIN'S SWEET SCENTS. —
Magnolia, White Rose, Frangipani, Geranium,
Patchouly, Ever-Sweet, New-Mown Hay,
and 1000 others.

Other ads touted products like Piesse & Lubin's Hungary Water ("Stimulates the Memory and invigorates the Brain"), which they proclaimed was first distilled in 1550 by Paracelsus Piesse, "the Alchymist Physician of Transylvania." An interesting notion, especially since Septimus Piesse was the English-born son of a War Office clerk. But he'd always had a flair for the dramatic and the fanciful. In one book, Piesse claimed that he had four sons with names beginning with the initials N, S, E, and W—the points of the compass. When not studying optics and analytical chemistry, their patriarch amused himself by learning useful skills . . . how to set ice on fire, for example. Or, better still, how to hear music with his ears plugged: with a long rod placed on a piano and the other end clenched in his teeth.

But it was as the world's foremost perfumer that Septimus Piesse won fame. The Laboratory of Flowers, his lavish store at 2 New Bond Street, held three floors fragrant with the bounty of Piesse's farms in Surrey and Provence; as a centerpiece for London's Great Exhibition of 1862, the firm even built a Fountain of Perfume that flowed with scented water. Their flagship store on New Bond Street was so busy that one boy's sole job was cutting off lengths of scented ribbon for customers. And so it came to pass that Piesse was universally known as the expert on such wares: his 1855 tome, *The Art of Perfumery*, went through multiple editions and translations, becoming the standard reference for perfumers for decades afterward.

It is a very strange book. Introducing his system for classifying and arranging perfumes, Piesse explains:

> There is, as it were, an octave of odours like an octave in music; certain odours coincide, like the keys of an instrument. Such as almond, heliotrope, vanilla, and clematis blend together, each producing different degrees of nearly the same impression . . . [and] semi-odours, such as rose and rose-geranium for the half-note: petty grain, neroli, a black key, followed by fleur d'orange.

Imagine rows of aromatic beakers like keys on a piano, played in musical scales. Arrange the scents into sweetly consonant chords—octaves, fourths, and the like—and pleasant music results. Arrange them into dissonant intervals, and your music literally *stinks*. Fortunately, Piesse worked out the aromatic scales, and *The Art of*

Perfumery contains pages of the complete bass and treble clefs of scent.

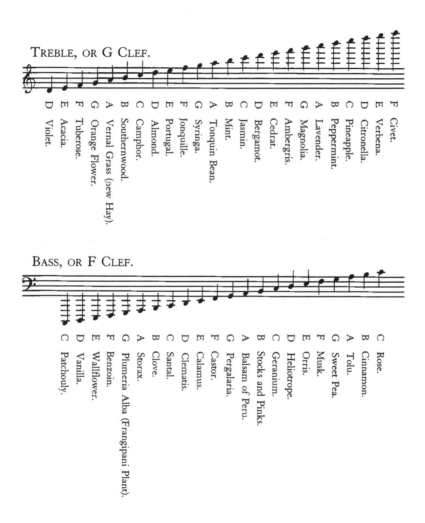

TREBLE, OR G CLEF.

F	Civet.
E	Verbena.
D	Citronella.
C	Pineapple.
B	Peppermint.
A	Lavender.
G	Magnolia.
F	Ambergris.
E	Cedrat.
D	Bergamot.
C	Jasmin.
B	Mint.
A	Tonquin Bean.
G	Syringa.
F	Jonquille.
E	Portugal.
D	Almond.
C	Camphor.
B	Southernwood.
A	Vernal Grass (new Hay).
G	Orange Flower.
F	Tuberose.
E	Acacia.
D	Violet.

BASS, OR F CLEF.

C	Rose.
B	Cinnamon.
A	Tolu.
G	Sweet Pea.
F	Musk.
E	Orris.
D	Héliotrope.
C	Geranium.
B	Stocks and Pinks.
A	Balsam of Peru.
G	Pergalaria.
F	Castor.
E	Calamus.
D	Clematis.
C	Santal.
B	Clove.
A	Storax.
G	Plumeria Alba (Frangipani Plant).
F	Benzoin.
E	Wallflower.
D	Vanilla.
C	Patchouly.

Hold a bass octave of two Gs with your left hand on the piano and play a G chord with your right. What would that smell like? Piesse knows:

Bouquet of Chord G

Bass.

G	Peregalaria.
G	Sweet Pea.
D	Violet.
F	Tuberose.
G	Orange Flower.
B	Southernwood.

Treble.

Piesse revolutionized perfumery. His odophone, a sort of candelabra for arranging scents into musical intervals, became an essential tool for perfumers. Millions who have never heard of Piesse still quote him when they speak of a scent's "base note"; it is the language of music, for Piesse did indeed think it was a note. He had coined the phrase to indicate the key a scent was in. The term persists because Piesse's music proved a very clever and useful metaphor.

But some took it literally. The June 1922 issue of *Science and Invention* magazine features this curious article entitled "The Smell Organ":

An entirely new organ has been developed, which instead of inspiring and thrilling audiences by sound, translates music into corresponding odors . . . atomizers are actuated by keys on the piano. Pressure upon any of these keys activates a circuit, which operates a solenoid, or suction type magnet, the latter releasing a valve and permitting compressed air from an air compressor and storage tank to blow the odorous vapour upward.

Like the carefully placed speakers in modern cinema, the concert hall positioned rotary fans to give the audience surround-smell. Between songs, ionizers wafted out a palate-cleansing breeze of ozone.

The smell organ was only the latest in a long line of similar instruments. The Jesuit scientist Louis Castel compared sound and color in the great color theory work of the eighteenth century, *Optics of Colors*; to press the point home, he invented an "ocular harpsichord" strung with colored ribbons in the place of wire. By the early 1900s, both the British art professor A. M. Rimington and the Russian composer Alexander Scriabin were independently building and playing, respectively, the colour organ and the chromola. Rimington's used massive arc lights to shoot out thirteen-thousand-candlepower beams, their colors corresponding to the notes pressed. Perhaps a few in the audience, bathed in the full spectrum of the colour organ, had their senses transported even further. After all, Francis Bacon had noted three centuries earlier that *rainbows smell*.

"I don't *compare* it to brown," Alex Van Halen once berated an interviewer inquiring about the sound of his snare drum. "It *is* brown."

It was his guitar-hero brother, Eddie, who became famous for "the Brown Sound," a metallic roar born of a jaw-dropping array of effects pedals, customized amps, and many a day spent in the Van Halen basement with a soldering iron. The sound Eddie was emulating was not like any other guitarist's—it was not, in fact, like any guitar at all. It was the tone of his brother's snare drum. Before switching band chairs, Eddie was the drummer and Alex the guitarist; later, on opposite instruments, each was still trying to capture the other's gestalt. What their two instruments shared was that tone—what the brothers have always flatly insisted is *brown*. Unless, of course, you are Septimus Piesse, in which case the open E on Eddie's guitar is just as irrefutably the smell of acacias.

Synaesthesia—literally "joined sensation," a synchronicity of senses—is one of the oldest phenomena known to neurology. "What a crumbly, yellow voice you have," one patient informed the great Russian psychologist L. S. Vygotsky; decades later, a writer in Australia insisted the name "Vancouver tastes like rice pudding but with raisins." For those with synaesthesia, vision may be conjoined with sound; the touch of a texture may generate a taste. The paired senses are constant and consistent, instinctive and involuntary. "I have never been destitute in all my conscious existence of a conviction that the letter E is a clear, cold, light-gray blue," admitted Dr. James Key in the 1880s. This synchronicity is present from early childhood; the most famous synaesthete, Vladimir Nabokov, complained as a toddler to his mother that the colors of the painted letters on his wooden blocks were "all wrong."

And these associations, even of the most fantastic variety, remain permanent. One teenage synaesthete, with a rare "audiomotor" form of the condition, twisted his body into different shapes depending on what words he was hearing. "When the doctor read the same list aloud ten years later," writes neurologist Richard Cytowic, "the boy assumed, without hesitation, the identical postures of a decade earlier."

Such pairings seem nonsensical, yet we are all prone to letting one sense interfere with another. The Virginia Dare food extract company once mischievously doped clear orange flavor extract with red food dye and then taste-tested the concoction on forty people. Most identified the flavor as cherry or strawberry; only five called it orange. Perhaps they were merely giving the answer they'd already expected: it was a red liquid, after all. But what can possibly explain the belief that a snare drum is inherently brown or that touching velvet tastes like butterscotch? The answer, like most in science, was a very long time in coming.

So I've wound up back in England for a few days to write a magazine article about a man who built fireproof houses in 1770s; he demonstrated how splendidly they worked by building models on Wimbledon Common and setting them on fire with volunteers inside. And they *did* work, fortunately. But I've taken the afternoon off from the London libraries to visit Redhill instead.

Redhill is on the Croydon-Portsmouth line and fairly undistinguished as suburbs go. It even rains there in a fairly undistinguished manner. Its rail office has the raffish look of futurism gone to seed; a scrum of bored teenagers huddle about outside, smoking awkwardly and watching the lights change at the knotty traffic intersection. I duck my head down against a gust of rain, dodge a few cars, and cross over to the local mall, a late-eighties berm of unimaginative brickwork. Inside is your typical British shopping center, all tile and ivy and escalators; I stroll past the Sanity video shop and then by Mad Cromwell's—this *is* the Belfry Shopping Centre, and its mascot *is* a bat, so one must expect madness-themed shops—and I wander past Exceptionails, where three bare-midriffed teens under bright man-icuring lights are being fumigated by nail polish vapor. The escalator takes me up—up above them, beyond the W. H. Smith, and on another escalator past the ever present green glow of the Marks & Spencer sign—and here I am.

Except I'm really nowhere. There are no stores on this third story: it is a gallery catwalk looking down mournfully upon the mall far below; this, presumably, is the belfry part of the Belfry Shopping

Centre. It leads nowhere except into a multistory car park. There is no one else up here, and my steps echo back to me with each step as I wander around the parking entranceways. I spy the small plaque affixed over one: ROYAL EARLSWOOD MUSEUM. It resembles a sign directing you to the loo.

And indeed there it is, hidden by an exit: a glass display case set into a wall, crowded with a jumble of old wooden items. THE GENIUS OF EARLSWOOD, reads a curatorial sign. A chatting couple steps through the car park doorway and then another; no one stops to notice me or the display case. They've seen it before, perhaps. Or maybe they never cared in the first place.

The July 1918 issue of *The Journal of Mental Science* has a centerfold, and Dr. Frederick Sano takes it off, takes it *all* off: the skull, the membranes, and the cerebrospinal fluid. He had removed them postmortem from the head of James Henry Pullen, the better to reveal the man's brain and its convolutional patterns. These were then carefully sketched by Sano in writhing foldout black-and-white drawings. Still, the doctor admitted, he'd been careless when storing the brain in a jar of hardening preservative: "The brain had not been suspended in the fluid during the first period of hardening, and had been lying on its inferior surface . . . exact measurements, therefore, could not be taken." This was a shame, because in 1918 it was still thought that brain weight and shape could tell you a great deal about someone. Even in its damaged state, though, Sano insisted in italics that he could see that "the orbital lobes were good, the corpus callosum was remarkable, and he was bound to have special capacity in the visual sphere of his mental existence."

Few readers would have disagreed with this assessment. Pullen, the "Genius of Earlswood Asylum," was Britain's most famous savant.

And if there was ever a place for a savant to seek sanctuary in 1850, it was Earlswood. The asylum's directing physician, J. Langdon Down, held that the "feeble-minded" could be taught—perhaps not taught much, and perhaps not quickly, but taught nonetheless. They could, on their own terms, become fully realized members of society. Earlswood was a remarkable exception in an era of institutional purgatories for the retarded, where most were doomed to be "transferred to the care of the various workhouses throughout the country, where they pass their lives without gaining an idea, and die like beasts of the field," as Dr. Andrew Wynter complained in 1876.

Down's asylum in Redhill was unlike any other Britain had ever seen, with a step-by-step five-year program to bring some measure of independence to each patient. After learning to hold utensils, they were progressively instructed with a graduated series of buttons, beginning with very large wooden ones down to the smallest clasps, in order to learn how to dress themselves. There was elaborate playacting for life in the outside world; an entire mock "shop" was set up inside the asylum and kept well stocked, with change in its till and with a shopkeeper's weights and measures—all so that patients could play shop and in the process learn how to count, to converse, and to function in ordinary village life. Such occupational training, an utterly ordinary part of therapy today, was revelatory in Down's time.

Down insisted that the patients be treated with respect; asylum staff were absolutely forbidden from corporal punishment and were to refer to inmates as "family members." Down lived on the premises, so the family metaphor was not a fanciful one. And they were a self-sufficient family: the sprawling complex had its own carpentry shop, its own farm, even its own print shop. All were run by the patients themselves. They also manned a cricket team and brass band. The whole arrangement was so far ahead of its time that Charles Dickens was known to visit simply for inspiration.

As helpless as many of them were when they arrived, the specific abilities of some patients defied belief. There was a young man who could recite Gibbon's *Decline and Fall of the Roman Empire* from memory; but if he stumbled over a word, he went right back to the beginning of the book and started reciting it all over again, as if *Decline* were an aria, with every note in its right place. Another patient had a preternaturally light touch and amused himself by peeling sheets of the *Daily Graphic* into tissue-thin plies. Others could inform you of the date of each patient's arrival and endlessly reel off train schedule information.

Not all of Down's patients were savants. Indeed, there were at least two groups: one was of extraordinarily sunny disposition, with some bodily and cranial anomaly and mild retardation. The other was darker, more impenetrable: almost invariably male, physically normal but prone to epilepsy, often possessed of perfect musical pitch, and so wildly variable in their abilities that retardation and genius might reside in the same man. The first group of patients Down famously dubbed Mongoloids, a name he later came to regret. Their condition is now known, more fittingly, as Down Syndrome. The other group was harder to fathom; if Down thought his first group vaguely resembled Mongolians, then the other was from an altogether undiscovered continent. And in that land, Pullen was clearly the king.

James Pullen arrived at the Earlswood Asylum in 1850, a boy of fifteen already written off as ineducable. He came from a respectable London family and yet barely spoke, barely seemed to hear at all.

Pullen was passionately fascinated by ships, though, and as a small child would fashion little boats out of any debris he could lay his hands on; indeed, he seemed to care only about drawing and crafting objects and was perversely withdrawn into his own world to an extent rivaled by one other boarder at the asylum—his own brother, William Pullen.

The Pullen brothers were captivated by engravings and would eagerly copy them out together onto sketch paper. William in particular excelled at this; in time, he became the lithographer of the asylum's print shop. But his talents were not given long to grow, as he died of cancer in his thirties. The younger Pullen was another story. His fascination with crafts bloomed into a sort of mad mastery: the carpentry shop, where he churned out everything from book-cases to walking sticks, was so constantly and jealously occupied by Pullen that it was finally ceded to him alone. To guard his work-shop, Pullen constructed a fearsome guillotine burglar trap, which might have worked had the staff not dismantled it. Undaunted, Pullen erected a fifteen-foot-tall mechanical monster to scare off any who dared interrupt his work; its glowering eyes, jaws, and bullhorn voice were operated by Pullen himself from a seat in its innards, where he controlled an intricate tangle of pulleys and levers.

Safe within his workshop, Pullen created an extraordinary array of art: intricate collages made of colored cigar-box bands, hand-hammered brooches, a forest of carved wooden implements. These he would take into Redhill to sell, in his eccentric and unspeaking manner, and he became a familiar sight to its residents. He knew precisely how much his items were worth and could not be cheated, for he kept a detailed notebooks of all the materials used in his work. On the other hand, he was not above trading an item for a wheel of good cheese from the local bailiff's wife.

But it was the creations he kept for himself that brought Pullen fame. They were largely ships: it had always been ships with him. Among his works is an extraordinary theological sculpture. His model of the universe was, of course, a ship: a Viking craft sprouting oars, with the angels and Satan manning alternate ends. The oars were worked by a clever rod assembly that Pullen built in, and out from the top of the ship emanated lightning bolts carved in ivory; the tusks were provided by none other than King Edward VII, who was so taken with Pullen's work that he regularly donated the valuable tusks from his hunts.

Pullen's greatest feat was still to come: an intricate model of Isambard Brunel's enormous steamer *The Great Eastern*. It was the most impressive ship of the time, and to Pullen—whom Down would take to the docks, knowing how he loved ships—the sight of *The Great Eastern* was revelatory. He spent three years building a facsimile of the ship; the planking alone required 1.2 *million* wooden pegs, all manufactured by Pullen in a woodmill of his own invention. The ship bore dozens of sail pulleys and cannon batteries; these were also forged by Pullen himself. The model won a bronze medal at the International Exhibition of 1872, and in later years Pullen would rather justifiably dress himself in an admiral's uniform for receiving such honors.

His fame grew so great that he eventually drew up a poster depicting his life story—an intricate cartoon of dozens of panels, all so that visitors needn't interrupt his work with questions. Instead, he'd silently direct them to the correct square on the poster. Among the panels is one depicting him as an unspeaking child, being thrashed by a frustrated tutor; the later ones are triumphant, set in his workshop amid his handmade creations.

Pullen's five-year term at the asylum passed, then another, then yet another. He never left. He was indeed quite untrainable in any conventional sense and yet also fiercely intelligent and gifted. He was not ready for the outside world but did not really belong with the other patients. So they let him stay. Pullen, alone of all the patients, was allowed to dine with the staff. He was still there after the asylum had moved to a new location at Normansfield Hospital, after Down himself had died, and after the doctor's sons had stepped in to run the asylum. And he was still there in 1913, sixty-three years after his admission, when the prominent neurologist A. F. Tredgold visited the still very much alive Genius of Earlswood. "Whilst showing me his handiwork he frequently stopped to pat his head and say 'Very clever,'" Dr. Tredgold mused. "And when I produced a tape-measure and asked permission to ascertain the extent of the cranial capacity he was delighted, and evidently regarded me as a very sensible person."

Pullen was right.

By the time I get to the Normansfield Hospital, dusk is approaching. The rain hasn't let up, and its miserable skies frame a solid three-story Victorian monolith. The windows and doorways are boarded up. The building has stood empty for many years now; after Down's family ran it for decades, it was turned into a national hospital and at length was abandoned. But signs promise that change is COMING SOON: they're building flats and semidetached houses here, and old wards are to be reworked into a hotel. The ailments of Down's patients live on, but the old treatments and asylums do not.

They did have some idea back then of what they were facing, for it was clear that many neurological conditions were hereditary. It is not merely the Van Halen brothers who both claim synaesthetic sound or the Pullen brothers who lived in their own world; such traits consistently run in families. It would surprise few neurologists now or then to hear that Nabokov's son was also synaesthetic or that Piesse's son later wrote his own treatise, *Olfactics and the Physical Senses*.

What is less easy to explain is why neurological phenomena cluster together. The autistic are prone to a constellation of oddities: synaesthesia, not at all coincidentally, happens to be one of them. Epilepsy, Tourette's, and perfect musical pitch all coincide with autism at a significant rate. *Why?* There had been unreadable clues here at Normansfield and elsewhere: in that wild visage of Peter the Wild Boy, in the drawings of an asylum inmate's brain, in the invitations of Septimus Piesse to the mysterious Chromophone. But it took another century to acquire the tools to interpret them.

With the advent of MRI and PET scans, it became possible to map synaesthetic brains in action. Patients with word-color associative synaesthesia were placed in a PET chamber, where they listened to a series of words. The monitors revealed what had long been suspected: both the language and visual centers of the brain were lighting up. A tangible and physical connection was occurring in the brains of synaesthetes. "Activity in visual areas occurred in the absence of any direct visual stimulation," one research team reported, "suggesting an unusual anatomical connectivity between language and visual areas."

So why was this happening? The better question is why it does *not* happen in the rest of us. In the first two years of life, the human brain forms neural connections at a furious rate; many of the neural pathways are useless or irrelevant, products of the bewildering flood of data coming into an infant brain and the tremendous rate of physical growth inside the cranium. Surprisingly, between the ages of two and three, the number of neurons in the brain shrinks. As useful pathways are established, "neural pruning" disposes of re-dundant and illogical ones—including, apparently, neural pathways connecting what should be disparate senses. Before pruning, we may all be synaesthetic. In synaesthesia, and in other phenomena such as perfect pitch and Tourette's, some of this neural pruning might not be occurring.

Tredgold and Sano, armed with scales and tape measures, were on the right track, for the effect becomes physically noticeable in the autistic. The excess of neurons is so great that their brains can actually be *heavier* than those of the neurotypical. The brain is like the walls of an old house, filled with disused wiring from earlier days: imagine if those lines were all left live and uncapped so that a great cross-wired mass of electrical impulses poured in. Synaesthesia is the neurological equivalent of switching on the kitchen lights and simultaneously setting off the blender. In autism, it is the equivalent of flicking on the light switch and blowing out the bulb. When autists flap their hands and thrash about, it is to protect themselves. They are being shocked by their senses.

CHAPTER 11

I WANT

It's a plain white office three-ring binder, with the words in block letters on the cover: I WANT. Inside are the rows of Velcro fastened and laminated cards, each with Jennifer's colored-pen drawings. *Outside. Banana. Grapes. Pizza. Sleep. Nurse. Macaroni and Cheese. Juice. Popcorn.*

Barb passes the folder back to us. "How's he been responding?"

"It's working, kind of. He's not saying the words yet . . . I mean, he'll repeat them when we say them first."

"He read most of *Green Eggs and Ham* out loud last night," Jennifer adds. "But I couldn't get him to ask for a Popsicle."

"So he's not initiating verbal requests."

"No. But he now hands us the cards when he wants something."

"That's great! That's fantastic. Seriously. He's understanding that you don't already know what he wants. It's drawing him out."

I look around the classroom. We've arrived early for Morgan's pickup, and the class isn't over yet; they're still cycling through their daily routine of teaching assistants watching the kids bounce and flap around in the gym; of the occupational therapist guiding them through going to the bathroom, or gripping a crayon correctly, or dressing themselves; of Barb leading the children into draping Koosh balls across their tummies and being held gently by the sides to get them past their touch aversion; of Bruce sitting one-on-one facing each boy to snap him out of his reverie, to respond to others by asking them about a table covered with wooden blocks—"Where is the red rectangle?"

A teaching assistant leads Dylan past us, and Barb watches them pass.

"Hi, Dylan! We'll be starting circle time soon." She turns back to us. "Do you want to sit with Morgan?"

"We won't be in the way, will we?"

"Getting in the way is the point. Otherwise they get locked into whatever they're focusing on. We want them to be aware of the people around them, to take turns, to respond. For some reason music is what usually gets through first, before anything else."

Another teaching assistant leads Morgan into the classroom.

"Hi, Morgan!" Jennifer says. "Hi!"

He glances at us, then looks away.

"Tigger plays a gold trombone," he responds. "Piglet plays—"

"Morgan," Barb says, stopping his memorized soliloquy, "let's check our schedule."

Morgan says nothing but holds her hand as she leads him to the activity marker on the wall. He drops a chip into the cup.

"Circle time! That's right. Good job, Morgan. Time to sit in the circle."

The four children sit on mats in a semicircle around Barb; Kwame smiles brightly at us and at everyone else; Nathaniel starts to cry. Morgan sits in front of us, holding forth on how Piglet plays a silver tuba. All the children have a grown-up sitting behind them, arms encircling them, watching and listening.

"Okay," Barb says, and waves a card marked SONG around to the group. "It's song time."

She grabs a plastic tray of toys—a bus, a fish, a star, a monkey—and holds it out to Nathaniel. He stops crying for a moment.

"Nathaniel, can you pick a song? Pick one."

He sobs a little at this.

"It's okay." An assistant behind Nathaniel guides his hand out to the plate. "Pick one."

Nathaniel grabs the monkey.

"Three little monkeys!" Barb smiles. She turns to a display of cards on the wall—THREE LITTLE MONKEYS; TWINKLE, TWINKLE, LITTLE STAR; THE WHEELS ON THE BUS; and SLIPPERY FISH—and detaches the first card.

"Three little monkeys, jumping on the bed . . ." She holds out three fingers as she starts to sing. A couple of the children join in, and where one falters and stops another sometimes picks up; the adults hold all their little hands and work them through the motions of the song. Each child picks out an object and a song in turn; and when they have all finished, Barb picks one last card off the wall. GOOD-BYE.

"Good-bye, Dylan, good-bye, Kwame, good-bye, Nathaniel, good-bye, Morgan," she sings. "Good-bye good-bye good-bye. Dylan, your turn."

"Good-bye," he sings, going through everyone's names. Kwame smiles at his turn but won't talk; Nathaniel cries but then unexpectedly stops and mumbles, "Nathaniel."

"Good job, Nathaniel! Morgan, your turn. Good-bye . . ."

Morgan won't be coaxed. The adults sing, Dylan and even Kwame join in, and Nathaniel hums a little. But Morgan stares at Barb, and then back at us, and then out the window; I cuddle him, and Jennifer sings into his ear, rocking him back and forth. The song finishes—"Good-bye!" Barb says cheerily—and parents come in to pick up their children. Morgan curls up between Jennifer and me, staring into the distance as the other kids around him are led away.

My face is right next to his, and I can just barely hear something amid the clatter of the emptying classroom.

"Goo-bye, Morgan, goo-bye, Dylan," Morgan breathes faintly. "Goo-bye goo-bye goo-bye."

He slaps a video into the VCR as soon as we get home.

"We . . . are . . . look . . . for . . . boos . . . coos . . ."

Morgan trampolines back and forth between the two mattresses in our bedroom—his little bed and our big bed—breathlessly singing along with his video. He knows every word of the tape. He can bounce like this for hours, and does; the entire house should be covered in bounceable elastic, as far as he's concerned.

And then a song comes on. He pauses, alarmed.

"Piano!" he yells.

Morgan grabs Big Bird and leaps off the bed, sprints into the living room, and throws the doll onto the piano bench. Then he scrambles onto the bench next to Big Bird.

"Whoo!" He pounds the piano keys.

Then he stops—listens—and batters away again.

"Oh yeah!" he howls. *"Shake it down!"*

Jennifer and I eye each other across the room.

"Where'd he get that from?"

"I have no idea."

"Yeahhhh!" He mashes out a rumbling pile of bass notes.

We smile, and I sit down to read my book in the gales of dissonance, and Jennifer goes back to her knitting. And slowly the volume of the piano goes down, too: down from two fists smashing the keys to one, from three notes to two, from two notes to . . .

ting ting ting . . . ting.

He won't stop but just keeps going.

ting . . . tingting.

I look up and put down my book.

ting.

He is holding Big Bird's little plastic hand, waiting for the right beat to tap the doll's hand onto the key.

ting.

"Jennifer?"

"Mmm?"

"Listen . . ." I nod over at Morgan.

He is focusing intently at one key, then on the sound of the TV— waiting for the right moment in the song.

Ting, he repeats. *Ting.*

Jennifer looks at me, puzzled. "What?"

Ting.

"Listen."

I shake my head in disbelief. "He's figuring it out."

His face is far away, his fingers insistent.

Ting.

His piano note repeats, like a lonely fragment of Morse code on a squalling radio.

Ting. Ting.

"The tonic note. He knows the key of the song."

"S-t-e-i-n-w-a-y."

"Good job, Morgan! That sp—"

"Ste . . . steen-eena-away."

"Steinway. That's right."

The shop owner turns from her apprentice to look out from the workshop at us, slightly worried.

"You okay there?"

"We're fine, thanks. Just looking."

The shop is crammed with old Bösendorfers, Baldwins, and Steinways in various stages of disassembly; one cabinet grand in the back of the store is splayed out into a veritable exploded drawing of piano parts. This is what I wanted him to see: roomfuls of pianos, their patinaed and stained and ivoried surfaces waiting to be brought into motion. Tuning tools lay scattered about on mismatched benches; Morgan's eyes are gleaming.

"Hammer . . ." He reaches into a Victorian parlor piano's exposed innards. "Hammers."

"That's right. Just like the ones at home," I ease his fingers back. "Gentle. You can touch the keys. Don't touch the—"

"Hammer . . ." He lunges in.

"No, no, gentle. Look. Look."

I guide his finger onto the middle C and tap it, while he watches the dirty felt-covered hammer lift up and smack the string. The piano is old and messed up, and the sound is wavery: *spoing, spoing.* He pushes my hand away and then presses the key himself. Then he reaches down and picks another C, an octave lower: *spoing SPOING spoing SPOING spoing.*

"Good job, Morgan! That's the same note!"

I feel eyes upon us.

"Marge . . ." The owner shakes my hand. "And this is my apprentice, Brenda."

A teenager waves quietly from across the store, half-hidden by an upraised piano lid.

"Hi," I wave back. "I'm Paul."

"Is he taking lessons?" The owner nods down.

"No, not yet."

"Hello," she says to him. "That's a big piano, isn't it?"

spoing. spoing. spoing.

"He's not a talker," I say.

"Ah."

spoing. spoing. spoing.

He stops and slowly presses a C down again, watching the mechanism inside the piano, waiting for it to engage. He is absolutely focused on it, fascinated.

"That's pretty neat, huh?"

A smile breaks across his face. He is beaming.

"And look, when you put your foot on this pedal—"

He lurches in and grabs the delicate hammers, wrenching them.

"Morgan, no! No no no. Gentle." I look over at the owner. "Sorry."

"That's okay."

But it's not, really. I try to guide him away from the piano. He shrugs me off.

"Morgan, let's get—"

He gives me a dismissive push without looking and continues to study the hammer mechanism.

"Honey, I know you want to take this apart, but—"

He flaps his hands angrily. I check my wallet to see if I have any ones on me.

"Ice cream."

"Ice cream!" he yells.

He bucks up and down on my shoulders as I piggyback him through the side streets, down and away from the piano store.

"Ice creeeeeam!" He bongos on my head.

"That's right." I turn my head up at him. "Ice cream."

The ice-cream parlor is nearly empty when we get there, just one other customer, which always makes things easier. We sit with our cones and eat them in contented silence broken only by the mix tape murmuring out of the employee area in the back.

"What a lucky boy!" says the woman at the next table.

Oh.

"Did your daddy buy you ice cream?" she asks at Morgan's back.

He eats in silence.

"Mint chocolate chip." I smile politely. "It gets his full attention."

A full minute passes. Then:

"It certainly does!" she chirps. "Look at him!"

"Yes," I smile, then turn back to him and wipe his chin. "Whoops. You're melting a little there."

He keeps eating as I wipe, looking briefly at me and then back at his cone.

"That really does have his attention."

Please, let us eat our ice cream.

"Yes, it does."

Please, please.

"How old is he?"

The questioner is maybe in her late forties herself, just a neighborhood woman in her blue raincoat, out to eat ice cream on a mild and drizzling day.

"Three."

"They're usually such chatterboxes at that age."

I smile and nod. "Yes."

"Look at him!"

"Yes."

"He's so serious!"

"Yes."

"Are you enjoying your ice cream?" she says to his back.

Pause.

"I'd say yes," I venture.

She doesn't stop.

"You see kids in here, usually they're bouncing off the walls. He's so serious! *Are you enjoying your ice cream?*"

Silence. Silence. Silence.

"*What's your n—*"

"He's autistic."

And it just sort of hangs there in the air for a second.

"He's not ignoring you," I explain, and stroke Morgan's hair. "It's just how he is."

She recovers pretty well, considering.

"Well, I . . . should . . . have . . . guessed! Oh. Do you know they have a program for deaf children at the neighborhood school here?"

"Yes, I hea—"

"I bet they work well with autistic children, too. He's so focused! I bet he'll be a tremendous learner."

"Yes, he is. He is."

Morgan keeps eating, content and unaware, and then stops to eye his cone carefully.

"Chocolate chip," he mutters, as if noting a butterfly genus. Then he bites the cone down to a stub and holds it out—not looking at me, waiting quietly for it to be taken away.

"All done? Okay."

I smile at the woman as we leave.

"You have a good day now," she says, and then blurts out: "Good luck."

"Thanks."

Outside I hoist Morgan onto my shoulders and we head home. We pass block after block of budding trees and slumbering Victorian houses—slowly leaning farmhouses with all the paint flaking away and primly restored bungalows. The back streets in Portland always feel impossibly quaint and sleepy on this kind of gray afternoon.

Now that there is no one else around, he decides to break his silence.

"A! B! C! D!" he sings out.

I crane my head up.

"E. F. G," I reply.

He bounces up and down on my shoulders.

"H! I! J! K!"

"L. M. N. O. P."

He leans all the way forward, so that his face hangs upside down in mine.

"Q! R! S!"

"T. U. V."

He grins maniacally at me. I can't even see where I'm walking.

"W! X!"

"Y and . . . Zeeee!"

He giggles and rubs his face in mine.

"You're a good singer," I tell him.

CHAPTER 12

We are now on our third doll. They don't even make them anymore—none of the stores quite knows how we got the first Talking Big Bird, since they haven't sold that model in years. I have to find one and then another on eBay to make surreptitious replacements; number one simply stopped working, and number two became dangerously unhinged, suddenly yelling about the color green at three A.M. Replacing them without Morgan noticing isn't easy. Big Bird goes everywhere now. If Morgan is eating food, he urges some into the bird's mouth; if he is drinking juice, he shoves the sippy cup into the fabric beak; if he is playing in the mud, Big Bird gets muddy, too. Now the third doll is aging rapidly; his fur is graying with dirt, his eye has a scratch across it, the magnetic blocks that click into his palm are becoming demagnetized.

Big Bird is losing his mind.

"Bricklejub! Redthyab!" he croaks weakly.

Morgan drags the doll by the scruff across the lawn and presses him into my lap. He is looking away but pushing the doll at me insistently.

"Honey?" I yell indoors. "Do we have extra batteries?"

"Kitchen drawer."

We carry the ailing doll inside and set him on the counter.

Morgan watches silently as I pull out the bird's innards, pop off the battery cover, and cram in a couple of new C cells. It makes an immediate difference.

"Bricklejub!" it roars. *"Redthyab!"*

"Um . . ."

"Brapthak!" it yells.

Morgan's eyes grow big and tear up; he flaps his hands, agitating.

"Morgan . . ." Jennifer tries to lead him away. "Morgan, do you want a cookie? . . . Morgan . . ."

"Hi! We can szerchmk!"

Morgan begins to keen, and Jennifer looks over at me. "Hide it."

I whisk the doll up a flight of stairs—*"Wheels bus grop regaff,"* it screeches—and hurl it to the back of a long walk-in closet filled with junk.

For a blissful moment, there is silence.

"Hi!" a voice gurgles out from the darkness. *"Do you want to play?"*

When I get back downstairs, all is quiet; Jennifer has taken Morgan to the bedroom and given him a deck of cards. But I can still see the doll's blocks scattered accusingly around the living room. *I have taken away his first friend.* There will be others; I think of the ones I saw whirring strangely to life outside London.

"Come in . . ." Professor Dautenhahn ushers me into her office. Like any professor's office, it is less a workspace than a conglomeration of piles of paper, all facing a computer and a chair. There is a *Far Side* cartoon taped to one shelf—she's a scientist, it's the law— and on her windowsill is what appears to be, well, a small shellacked roast turkey. I stare at it, trying to figure out what it is. Something fossilized?

"I am a biologist," she explains. Ah. "But my work has taken me into robotics and computer science."

Her voice is accented, and—is everyone working in autism a blond-haired Austrian?—as she clicks through her computer files, I look back out the office window. Everything in Hertfordshire is made of brick. The town of Hatfield has blocks of lowslung brick houses, skulking brick stores, a brick Catholic church, and—oh look!—a tree. Just kidding. That's brick, too.

Page after page churns out from a laser printer. She staples a sheaf and hands it to me. "This is one of our more recent papers," she says. *Games Children with Autism Can Play with Robota, a Humanoid Robotic Doll*: I leaf through it as we walk down the hallway. If computing seems made for autists, it's probably because computing was in no small part made *by* autists. And just as autistic adults have been inextricably intertwined with the invention and development of computing, PCs and autistic children were also meant for each other from the beginning; listed in the references is a paper entitled "Computers in the Treatment of Nonspeaking Autistic Children," published in 1971—the dawn of personal computing.

The university's comp sci center is humming along when we arrive; everyone is focused on their monitors and ignoring one another in a sociable sort of way. We pull a couple of chairs away from unused terminals, settle in front of a TV monitor, and pop a tape into the VCR.

"This is raw footage," she warns. "It's not edited yet, but it will give you an idea."

An image of an anonymous room flickers on, with a time code running at the bottom; a young boy of perhaps eight plays on the floor. Hands connected to an unseen adult set down an object: a squat, flat, four-wheeled platform with fragile sensor assemblies sprouting out of the top. It is not a humanoid, but rather a squarish silver vehicle.

"That is an early model of robot that we are using," she says, "and . . ."

The boy gazes at it, runs his fingers over the cold metal housing, gives a sensor a tentative poke, and then—tears it off.

"And, ah, that happened a lot."

The off-screen adult reaches in to reattach the sensor.

"The sensors are exposed." Dautenhahn points at the TV screen. "The connections are very fragile, and the autistic children pull them out. They want to look at them, figure them out. They're *very* interested in how things work. We've tried taping the sensors down, but they just pull them right out again."

"I imagined the robots would be more doll-like."

"Initially, we try to make the robots as simple as possible. You don't want the children getting distracted by little details; autistic boys will just focus on something small and you can't get them to engage with the entire mechanism."

This is one of the profound differences between autistic and neurotypical perception. Theirs is literally disintegrated—autists test remarkably well at assembling jigsaw puzzle pieces but may be unable to explain what it's picture of. In fact, some autists find it easier to assemble puzzles when the pieces are flipped over onto their blank side. The big picture is a distraction: broad relations go unnoticed in such a world, while subtle details are immensely magnified. Autists cannot see the forest for the trees or even the trees for the bark and leaves. They focus obsessively on the individual parts, trying to make sense of the mass of innumerable fragments of information, unable to take in the situation at a glance.

The monitor flickers and a new segment appears; now it is

another boy, huddled on the floor and chewing quietly on the collar of his fleece jacket.

"This child is not verbal," the professor says. "He is more severely autistic, not so social as the first child."

Yet he is far more interested in the robot when it appears. He crawls around it, peers in at its sensors, and curls on the floor around it. The robot sputters about a little on its weak motor, back and forth. The boy lays his head on the floor and beams at it, smiles gloriously at the contraption as it scoots straight up to his face. He *loves* it.

"We get some teachers who say that autistic children cannot cope with novelty. But look at this." She nods at the soundless video. "He's never seen this robot before, and he's not afraid of it at all. I couldn't lie on a floor and let a strange robot head straight at me."

Yet that is just what he does as the robot bears down on him, stopping just short of his face. He grins even more widely at this.

Dautenhahn fast-forwards to one last segment; now there are two boys.

"Now," she says, "this is the key step."

The boys examine the robot—but it is frozen.

"This is an important part of the design." She points at the soundless video. "The robot only responds to one set of commands at a time. The boys must take turns to use it, and therefore they must first acknowledge each other's presence. So that means . . ."

One of the boys sits back, and the other touches the robot. Now it responds.

"That boy has used the robot before on his own. Now look—he is explaining to the other boy how it works."

The other boy listens and then takes a turn.

"There. *That* is what we are working toward," she explains. "Not only is he engaging with the other child, but he understood that the other child did not know how to use the robot."

For him to understand this means just one thing—one very crucial thing. He is developing a theory of mind.

The robots slowly bump around in their plywood pens like blind kittens. Bump bump bump. They are made out of metal, plastic, even out of Legos.

"Very handy," one grad student explains from his computer. "Legos are brilliant."

The noise in the robot workshop is constant from their futile efforts at escape: but with each bump, they are learning. Professor Dautenhahn watches with her arms folded as Tami, a doctoral student, picks one up.

"This is our new robot, the one I'm working with," Tami says. It's a curved white plastic model, with a dark stripe of sensors on its sides. "It detects infrared movement, as well as dark and light."

"We need to pull the eyes off." Dautenhahn picks at the robot's face with a fingernail. "The eye stickers are not functional. Also, they might frighten the children."

But the stickers don't want to come off: for now, the robot gets to keep its freakish eyes. Tami places the robot back into its rectangular pen, and as she steps around the robot, it scurries to avoid her.

"We are trying to stimulate interaction through chasing activities—they chase it, it chases them back, and . . . well. Actually, it chasing them may be problematic." She pauses dryly. "Getting chased by a robot could be upsetting."

"Ah."

She takes another step at the robot, and it scoots away, back and forth, like a panicked mouse. Dautenhahn nods approvingly and picks a squat metallic robot out of a lab cabinet.

"Here's the model we used in the video," she says. "It's heavier than the new ones, but still light enough for children to pick up." She hands it to me, and I heft it in my hands. It comes under the weight category of Things I Don't Want Thrown at My Head.

There's another robot still in the cabinet, a sweet little pigtailed girl, but with a torso of servomotors and chips—an extra from Westworld, by the look of it. And I can't stop *looking* at it. A friend of mine in the advertising business was once confronted by a similar creature. It was a company's prototype of a talking doll designed to watch TV with your child and turn its cuddly lifeless head to converse. The grisly little toy was perched on a desk when it turned its unblinking stare upon him and said, in tones to freeze the blood—"Will you be my friend?" To my colleague's credit, he restrained himself from his immediate impulse—grabbing a desk stapler and beating the thing senseless—and limited himself to a full-body shudder.

There *is* something creepy about animatronic dolls. Sometimes the effect of a doll is comically wrong, as with early Victorian efforts like Vincent Lake's All-Steel Doll—oh, imagine the joy in your little girl's face when she finds that cold lump of metal under the Christmas tree! But usually the vacant stare of weighted glass eyes is just real enough to be unsettling. One robotics professor in Tokyo, Fumio Hara, has been developing progressively uncanny generations of "face robots," which can read a small range of emotions and imitate them with its expressive actuator muscles and smiling silicone dentures. One use for Hara's face robots, a few people have suggested, might be for autistic children. But it all seems a little nightmarish.

"That's Robota," Professor Dautenhahn says, following my stare. "This is the only one that looks like a human."

"Why's that?"

"Human faces are distracting." She passes the doll to me. "There is too much information, too much stimulation. Particularly for the younger autistic children. We've had some interesting results with a teenage girl using Robota. Younger children, they do not know where to begin when they see faces. They relate readily to mechanical devices. But humans . . ." She trails off.

I hand the robot back to Dautenhahn, and she sets its lifeless form back in the cabinet. She looks at it a moment.

"Humans," she says, "are a challenge."

Morgan is lolling back in my lap in our living room chair; we showered him earlier, and he's finally stopped being mad at us. He cuddles against me and draws on his Magna Doodle, the same pattern over and over—a shaky rendering of a circle atop a straight line.

He silently eyes his drawing.

"Periscope," he announces.

Periscope drawings turn up everywhere these days: in pen on construction paper pads, scribbled on the bedroom wall in crayon, on the floor in wet paint, in marker on a book cover, on his computer screen in yogurt, on his plate with string cheese and a Ritz cracker.

"*Periscope*," he repeats.

"You drew a periscope," I nod.

It is the periscope-shaped voice trumpet from *Teletubbies*: it fascinates him. On the show it is the parental voice, the voice of the outside world, compressed into a metal speaking tube that rises and sinks back into the ground throughout the day to wake up the

Tubbies, to issue commands, to sing them back to sleep. It is the parent rendered to the simplest terms—a stick figure that soothes, and commands, and makes sense of the outside.

He curls in closer to me and draws it again.

"Hysterical," the computer says.

Morgan clicks around through the software, already past a Cambridge University logo informing us that we are operating Mind Reading Version 1.0. Mind reading is a curious notion to be promulgated by Cambridge, perhaps, but it starts making more sense when you see that Simon Baron-Cohen is one of the creators. The mind reading is not of the "What number am I thinking of?" variety, but rather "What intention is my face conveying?" It is instinctive to most humans, so we hardly think of it, because we learn it automatically. Autists hardly ever think of it, either, for the opposite reason: many of them have never learned to interpret facial expressions, so it does not occur to them to look. To learn to judge social situations, they must do what they do best—memorize and systematize. That means software, with human faces broken down into 412 emotions, broken down into 24 emotive categories, and with video examples of the same emotion displayed by the young and old and by male and female actors.

One is curiously familiar.

Harry Potter?

And there he is: Daniel Radcliffe, minus his trademark glasses and owl. Here, away from the *Harry Potter* set, he looks like . . . well, any English boy, really.

"*Ugh*," he says. Raw squid is being held up to his face. The emotion, of course, is disgust. Radcliffe might not even have to do much acting to evoke that one: sensory researchers call rotting squid the worst naturally occurring smell in the world. Clearly Dr. Baron-Cohen and his assistants have done their homework.

Morgan squirms about on my lap and looks up at me.

"Look." I point at the screen. "Yucky!"

"*Yucky!*"

"Yucky!"

"Yuu-ahh . . ." He warbles his voice. "Keeey."

We take a gentle tour of hysteria. Hysteria is listed as a level four emotion, out of six levels of complexity, and when I click on a voice sample for hysteria, the software emits a mum's annoyed "Come on, let's go." True, that *is* about as hysterical as the British get. But in spite of the plummy accents, there remains a universality to the faces on-screen: the old woman smiling sweetly, the man who smiles not so sweetly, the child who shows disappointment. No matter who or where they are, the expressions are all more or less recognizable. You could indeed learn to read people from this.

But even for people who *can* intuit emotions, who know what they're looking at, the task is a daunting one: Darwin's 1872 opus, *The Expression of the Emotions in Man and Animals*, took decades of effort just to establish his basic thesis that, among man and beast alike, "the same state of mind is expressed throughout the world with remarkable uniformity." The mind reading software is a sort of *Expression* for our time, but for a purpose that Darwin could scarcely have imagined. Yet he was not so far separated from its new audience. Darwin's grandfather, the bookish ceramics artisan Josiah Wedgwood, had once examined one such curiously alienated and unsocialized man. He'd even mused that the fellow's head resembled that of Socrates. That man was, of course—well, it just had to be, didn't it?—none other than Peter the Wild Boy.

* * *

A final screen for each emotion shows a space provided for the autist to type in his or her own field observations. It reads:

People, places and times I have noticed this emotion.

And there they will keep records, like patient scientists studying the curious fauna of the earth, hoping to decipher this strange and contradictory species that somehow, absurdly, they are apparently a part of.

Morgan types merrily away at the keyboard, entering in his verdict:

ppppancake

It's been a favorite word of his lately. And why not?

The CD pops out, and I run my thumb over the title embossed upon it: "The Library of Human Emotions." There is something haunting in this metaphor. The first thing that comes to mind is an actual library, filled with dusty books, each one dedicated to infinitesimal gradations of human emotion. It is like something out of Borges—or, perhaps, Martian poetry. The "Martian school of poetry" was a fad in Britain in the late 1970s, based upon the clever Craig Raine poem "A Martian Sends a Postcard Home." It revolved around the conceit of an alien naïvely describing planet Earth and its mysterious phenomena:

Mist is when the sky is tired of flight
and rests its soft machine on ground:

then the world is dim and bookish
like engravings under tissue paper.

Rain is when the earth is television.
It has the property of making colours darker . . .

The book made Raine famous—for a poet, anyway—and then went out of print. The Martian school of poetry started showing up in anthologies for children, though, which is only fitting: the idea of observing a curious and yet seemingly arbitrary world might be the only poetic conceit that truly makes sense to a child. But Martian poetry now also lives on, perhaps, in the notes-taking page of autistic software.

Come to think of it, Baron-Cohen did make a rather curious comment to me when I was leaving his home in Cambridge. "Have you seen *Martian in the Playground?*" he mused. "It's interviews with autistic schoolchildren, and it's written by an autistic woman. Some people might think the title offensive, but . . . in fact, it was their own title. It's very evocative."

He's right. Autists are described by others—and by themselves—as aliens among humans. But there's an irony to this, for precisely the opposite is true. They are us, and to understand them is to begin to understand what it means to be human. Think of it: a disability is usually defined in terms of what is missing. A child tugs at his or her parents and whispers, "Where's that man's arm?" But autism is *an ability and a disability*: it is as much about what is abundant as what is missing, an overexpression of the very traits that make our species unique. Other animals are social, but only humans are capable of abstract logic. The autistic outhuman the humans, and we can scarcely recognize the result.

PART FOUR

SAFETY IN NUMBERS

CHAPTER 13

It's an uphill walk to the Bancroft Library in Berkeley, but you will find distractions along the way: the little deli with the big ice-cream freezer, the board-game shop crammed with the inevitable war-geek games, the crowded coffeehouse facing out onto the perpetually jaywalked crossing over to campus. Take the foot-bridges over Strawberry Creek—a pleasant little brook if you don't mind the occasional hint of tritium seeped out by the nuclear lab—get past the fifth-degree questioning of the librarian clerk at the rare-book room, sift through the holdings of the Regional Oral History Office, and eventually you can find yourself sitting and listening to a taped interview with Arthur Schawlow, who won a Nobel Prize for helping to invent the laser in the late 1950s.

But on side A of tape 12, he is not talking about Bell Labs, where his famous experiments took place, or about his later years in California as a college professor. He is talking about his son Artie. Artie, he explains, loved to swim. But the Schawlows would get early morning calls from neighbors: Artie was out there, joyfully swimming in their backyard pools. They couldn't explain to their son when he could and couldn't do it: even after putting up a fence and covering doors with hooks and locks, sometimes he'd bolt from the house while they were sleeping—not out of rebellion, particularly. He just wanted to swim.

The interviewer asks Schawlow if he and his son had any real communication: Schawlow's voice on the tape begins to choke up. *No*, he says—*No*. They were trying, but there were so many things they were not to know: Schawlow and his wife were parents of an autistic child in an era when their Stanford psychiatrist was wrongheadedly interested in positing how Artie's mother had psychically ruined her child. But what *should* one be doing to communicate? It is a damnably hard question. Autists do not see their lives as a riddle: they make sense to themselves. Yet to anyone else, communication with an autist can seem like an unsolvable enigma, and both must struggle to make themselves understood.

Sometimes it works. "In all the annals of human heroics," wrote the paleontologist Stephen Jay Gould a few years before his death, "I find no theme more ennobling than the compensations that people struggle to discover and implement when life's misfortunes have deprived them of basic attributes of our common nature." He was writing of a young man named Jesse, an autistic savant who had developed a fearsome facility with numbers—one not entirely unlike Gould's own fascination with baseball statistics. Jesse is a mental calculator of dates: give him any date, and he will tell you what day of the week it fell on. Gould was curious to see if Jesse understood why the number 28 was an important number to date-calculating savants: it's because calendars repeat every twenty-eight years. But when Gould asked Jesse about the significance of the number 28, the savant only replied with a seeming non sequitur.

"Five weeks."

Gould racked his brain trying to imagine what this could mean.

Or was it simply meaningless, part of the autist's repetitive collage of found noises and words?

"I understood in a flash several hours later," Gould later wrote, "and his solution was so beautiful that I started to cry."

Jesse *was* trying to communicate. Rather than the convoluted algorithm that Gould had worked out to try to understand date calculation, Jesse had used an elegant bit of arithmetic. Counting using a fifty-two-week year always leaves one or two extra days each year; after twenty-eight years, one always has thirty-five extra days, which divided by seven means an even five weeks: so twenty-eight years is the first interval that always has identical days of the week for the same two dates, past and present.

If Gould was brought to tears by the intellectual beauty of Jesse's answer, I imagine he was moved even more by the reaching out that it represented.

"He is my firstborn son," he wrote, "and I am very proud of him."

"Hello. I'm Mars."

Morgan is standing precariously on the arm of a chair, watching me make a sandwich in the kitchen as he cycles through an entire five-minute-long chunk of dialogue from *Blue's Clues*.

"Hello," he adds. "I'm Jupiter."

"Hey, Morgan." I abandon the kitchen and pull a sketch pad out of his toy box. "Do you want to draw the planets with me?"

"Saturn has icy rings," he continues, but clambers down to see what I'm doing.

I draw a circle and rings and write out "SATURN" underneath it.

"Saturn," he reads. He grabs my hand and pushes it into the pad.

"You want another picture?"

"Hello, I'm Uranus," he says. "Uranus spins on its side."

"Okay, Uranus," I say as I start drawing. By the time I get done with a crude chiaroscuro of the oddly vertical belting of that planet's cloud cover, he's lost interest and walked away to stare out the living room window. I go back to the kitchen and finish making his sandwich and then set it next to him. He picks up a wedge of the sandwich without looking away from the window.

"Morgan, do you want to go outside?"

"You want to go outside," he repeats through a mouthful of bread and peanut butter.

"All right." I pull together my dadly assemblage of baby wipes and change and keys while he scarfs down the rest of his food. "Let's go outside."

Once we get out into the sun, he wants to be on my shoulders.

"Morgan, do you want to go to the playground?" I hoist him up. "The playground?"

He is humming aimlessly to himself.

"The playground? Morgan, do you—"

Hmmm mmm mmm hmmm hmmm.

"How about the park?"

Hmmm mmm mmm hmmm hmmm.

I am walking up to the intersection near our house and have to decide where we're going; he's not given any indication of what he wants to do.

"Oww—" He wrenches my head to the left, as though it's the steering wheel of a big rig. "Okay, we'll go that way."

He steers me to a bus stop, bouncing with excitement as a Tri-Met bus approaches, and I get my change out. Not many people get excited by the prospect of a ride on public transit, I suppose. Actually, no, that's not true: some people do. One of Morgan's schoolmates has been memorizing the local bus schedules.

There is a strange pleasure to schedules, I will admit. I felt stricken, back when we lived in San Francisco, when their besieged bus system stopped issuing schedules altogether. The fat folded timetables had traditionally sat untouched in their TAKE ONE displays near the front of the car. Anyone consulting them was sure to be a tourist; no city resident was naïve enough to actually plan their day around the times. Yet the mere existence of the schedules meant something. They were an acknowledgment that some kind of order lurked within the workings of the city—or had once, maybe long ago, and perhaps even then only in theory. But it was a reassuring gesture, and even the useless updates had a certain pleasure to them.

"Everyone is a virtuoso on his own instrument," the novelist Thomas Bernard once wrote, "but together they add up to an intolerable cacophony." The world of people and the traffic that carries them is chaotic: a schedule orchestrates it into a thing of everyday beauty. The ever changing arrays of timetables that transit systems create are variations on a numeric fugue, and you can watch them develop like a piece of music moving through a chord progression.

The bus doors slam open, and I carry Morgan inside. "Three little monkeys, jumping on the bed," he sings loudly in my lap as we ride down Hawthorne. I mime the song with his hands in mine. I'm glad he picked "Monkeys," since he also likes yelling out the song title "Clap and Laugh"—only when he says it, it comes out as the Zen-like "Crap and Laugh." Our bus passes the old Masonic temple and the 1920s movie palace where we sometimes take Morgan to see cartoons for the hour or so before he gets too antsy to stand it; on the other side of the street the bookstores and coffee shops slide by, and then the bakery, and Morgan presses his face against the window to

watch, singing all along. Three little monkeys . . . two little monkeys
. . . one little . . .

"I feel all alone."

I jerk my head back. Morgan is smiling strangely, staring out the
window, and singing . . . God, I don't know. *I fee ahh ah-yohn.* It
can't be what it sort of sounds like . . .

"I feel all alone," I hear. "I feel all aloooone . . ."

"Morgan . . ." I hold him tighter. "Sh-sh-shh. Daddy's right
here."

"I feel all aloooone," he sings loudly.

I look up and nobody's really looking, yet I feel horrified: It is the
first original sentence he's ever spoken and *it's this.*

"I feel all a-looone . . ."

"Sh-sh-shh. It's okay, it's okay."

He pays no heed to me; he seems unfazed and sings louder.

"Morgan," I start, "do you want to sing 'Three Little Monkeys'
again?"

"I feel all alone."

"Three little monkeys ju—"

"I feel all alone."

He's now yelling it out, and we dodge out of the bus at the next
stop, and I hurry him homeward, toward the ice-cream shop, toward
the toy store, toward anything at all. He is skipping alongside me.

"I feel all a-looone . . ."

"Morgan . . ." I pick him up. "Look at me. Honey, look at me.
I'm right here. Daddy's right here."

"I—"

"Look—" I grab a bus schedule out of my pocket, where I'd
stuffed it on the bus as a distraction. "Look at the numbers on here.
Pretty neat, huh?"

He stops yelling and examines the schedule intently.

"Two thirty-five," he finally says.

I carry him home, holding him tightly as he clutches the number 14 schedule.

Timetable creation is a subset of math—specifically, of operations research or combinatorial optimization. But the timetables are not really meant to be precise. "Trams in cities often have a timetable," a mathematician once informed me patiently, "while everybody knows that they should only be taken seriously for the frequency that they imply." But they are comforting in their familiar logic, and each minor revision creates a hint of novelty.

Collecting schedules takes a peculiar form of devotion. But there are, in fact, timetable collectors all over the world. There's the Düsseldorf-based Internationalen Interressengemenischaft der Fahrplansammler; one can only hope that they refer to themselves with an acronym. America has the National Association of Time-table Collectors, which has held steady at about 500 members (virtually all male) for decades now. The American group even holds a yearly convention; last year's was a two-day event at a Cincinnati Holiday Inn. Brit schedulists can thumb through hard-cover reissues of *The Bradshaw Railway Timetable*—that's correct, these are reprints of outdated schedules—and if the fancy grabs them, they can also join a Transport Ticket Society, which saves the stubs from journeys. The British have collected ticket stubs for centuries; even before railways were invented, some collected used turnpike tickets. In another hemisphere altogether, you can join the Australian Association of Timetable Collectors.

The AATC has two newsletters, including one called, inevitably, *Table Talk*. It makes for strangely touching reading; you realize how used collectors are to getting strange looks for their hobby. One 1998 issue featured this letter from Derek Cheng, an immigrant from Hong Kong who is described as one of their youngest members:

> Three years ago I didn't even know what a timetable looked like. Now I am just mad about this creature. I have timetables for 1,966 bus routes around Australia. Originally from Hong Kong, I had no knowledge about timetables. The transport operators there do not publish them.

At school, he says, he is mocked for his "stupid and silly" pursuit— but among fellow timetable collectors, he feels at home.

There's safety in numbers.

Morgan clambers into Jennifer's lap on the living room sofa and presses the Magna Doodle into her hand.

"One," he says.

"You want me to write the number one?"

"One."

"Okay, then." She writes "1" down and then puts a single dot underneath it to indicate the quantity. He immediately erases it.

"Two," he says.

She makes a number 2 and then two dots; and I watch them while I sweep the floors and they continue their numbers up into the thirties. Morgan's at 32 when he pauses suddenly.

"One," he says again.

"One!" Jennifer writes it down. Morgan eyes the number curiously, smiles, and grabs the pen from her. He makes some markings.

"Paul?" she says. "Come look at this."

I set the broom aside and look at the battered Magna Doodle. He has added two dots and a curve—eyes and a mouth.

Morgan erases it.

"Two." He smiles and alters it again.

"Three."

"Morgan, that's great! What a good face!"

He smiles and then turns back to business.

"Four."

Eeek. Eeek. Eeek.

He's bouncing on the bed, and the springs are protesting underneath. We've wrecked one mattress this way already and are well on the way to trashing a second. He weighs barely forty pounds yet, but he bounces on them for an hour or two a day: bouncing up high, then low, then pulling pile driver moves and side bounces. There are two beds in the bedroom—our king-size and his twin—and one of his favorite things in the world is popping in a videotape and then watching it while ricocheting back and forth across the room. He's bopping around while watching a kid's show about cooking.

"Let's roll out the crust to go on top," it chatters.

And then he begins again.

"I feel all alone."

"Oh, Morgan . . ."

"I feel all a-looone."

"Now it's time to bake the pie!" the TV chirps.

I reach out for Morgan, but he's bouncing away to the other bed, flapping his hands.

"I feel alll a-looone."

I am becoming distraught.

"Morgan, sh-sh-shhh . . ."

"I feel all alone."

I try to hold him and comfort him, but all he wants to do is trampoline back and forth between the beds, flapping his hands and turning somersaults. He is smiling as he says it, and *it is freaking me out*. I feel all alone—I feel all alone—and I cannot help him. And then, suddenly: I hear the music from the TV. It is rising and falling in time with my son's yelling.

"Ay fee ah ay-yohn," Morgan sings along. He is . . . he is *singing with the tape*. He is singing along with a child on the video—and, as he will do, he has altered each syllable of the chorus so many times over that only a few phonemes and cadences remain.

This is what he is saying:

Pastry all day long!
Pastry all day long!
Pastry all day loo-oooong!

I slump back onto the bed. It has nothing to do with feeling alone—
nothing to do with existential despair—and a great deal to do with
being three years old.

He's the happiest child I've ever seen. Yet there isn't a day
when I don't worry, when I don't have a sudden stab in the gut
that someday, when we are gone, when he is an old man, he
might really feel alone. You worry how your children will get on
in the world even after you're gone, even after they're older than
you yourself are today; I suppose every parent worries about this.
Yet autists face so many more worries—that, in a world of their
own, they may come to feel lonely, depressed, utterly isolated—
and that you may not be there to help them. Who can be there
for them?

"Pastry . . . all . . . day . . . long."

Morgan glances over at me, smiles, and keeps bouncing.

It's late, and Morgan drifted off to sleep hours ago. Jennifer is up
working on a canvas: it's a painting of mermaids watching TV.

"So my checkup is tomorrow," she says. "Should I ask her?"

"Yeah . . . yeah, let's ask."

"I mean, if we can't, if she doesn't think we should . . ."

"We could adopt," I say.

"We could. In any case, I don't want Morgan to be an only child."

"Going into the world alone is tough for anyone."

"But if she says we can go ahead . . ." She paints a long wispy line.
"There's a chance."

"I heard four percent," I sit up. "But no one really seems to know for sure."

Four percent.

Firstborns appear more likely to be autistic, as are boys. If we decide to have a second child, particularly if we have a girl, the chances are something like 4 percent or less. All kinds of figures get thrown around, though; maybe the real figure is higher. But what does that kind of figure mean? Four percent . . . any percent . . . of what? The significance of 4 percent is another way of asking: would you do this all again?

Well?

Jennifer mixes more paint on her palette, bringing out a darker blue for the background of her painting. Behind her, piled up near our front door, is a small mound of shoes thrown together haphazardly: mine, hers, Morgan's, all jumbled up into big feet and little feet and littlest feet. There's probably two dozen shoes there.

One shoe: 4 percent.

"What are your mermaids watching?" I ask.

"Judge Judy."

Jennifer eyes the hue of the paint she's mixed, looks over her painting, and then sets down her palette.

"I'm ready for it," she says.

I nod.

"I am, too."

CHAPTER 14

I still remember it perfectly, though it happened maybe five years ago now: a man, blind, walking behind his guide dog on a shady little back street in San Rafael on a California summer afternoon. And I remember the car approaching up the street.

It was not stopping.

"Hey!" I roared.

The car stopped: the man looked up. Everything stood still a moment.

"We're training him," he said blankly.

The woman driving gave me a little wave; and then I looked down and saw the Seeing Eye logo on her car.

"Oh . . ." I reddened. "Right."

They went back to work, and I walked quickly away. They understood what I had done, and I understood what they were doing: everyone knows what a guide dog is and that they have to be trained to help people through traffic and that sort of thing. But it was not always such an intuitive connection for people to make.

The title of Hector Chevigny's 1946 memoir would do Dalí proud. You could display it at a county fair with a giant stuffed teddy bear as a prize, and no one would correctly guess what the hell it's about.

That's probably one reason it's been out of print for fifty years. But let me assure you—*My Eyes Have a Cold Nose* is worth reading.

"Just how does a dog lead you, and how does he know where to go?" Chevigny asks. "It seems incredible that anyone would dare try crossing Lexington Avenue at high noon with only a small animal to guide him." He had a good reason for worrying: the forty-year-old screenwriter's retinas had detached the year before, leaving him suddenly and totally blind. Facing the prospect of his life depending on a dog with the not entirely reassuring name of Wiz, he considers ordering "an ambulance to be standing on the corner of Lexington and 51st Street—just in case."

The notion of the disabled utterly relying on a pooch for much of anything was still fairly new. Guide dogs were born out of the horrors of World War I: with thousands of German soldiers blinded by mustard gas, phosphorus flashes, and flying shrapnel, schools for guide dogs started opening across Germany and Switzerland in the early 1920s. The first German shepherd guide dogs simply . . . well, shepherded. They walked the veterans among well-marked and established paths, nosing them along and keeping them from wandering. From these humble beginnings came the orange-vested dogs that lead the blind across streets, alert the deaf to honking horns and ringing doorbells, and fetch for the parapalegic. But man's best friend really does need to be a friend: if you hate dogs, they will not guide you.

"The dogs are not trained to work for the blind, they are *persuaded*," Chevigny notes. "The dogs cannot be fooled."

If you were looking for a close second in the obscure-book-title contest, *A Cow's Eye View* would come in just behind *My Eyes Have a Cold Nose*. Fortunately, this title was changed before publication, and

Thinking in Pictures now has little chance of being forgotten. Temple Grandin's autistic autobiography is what Helen Keller's memoir was for the deaf and blind: it introduced the rest of the world to a vast and previously unknown realm of lived experience. That realm, to the neurotypical reader of Grandin, is autism. But that is not an unknown realm to Grandin: to her, it's simply ordinary life. Her abiding passion for exploration is in the behavior of animals. Her book's original title, ungainly as it was, is a direct window into her purpose.

"When a well-respected animal scientist told me that animals do not think, I replied that if this was true, then I would have to conclude that I was unable to think," she writes. Autists—written off as feral or animal-like in past eras—do indeed have an intensely acute focus and nonconversational perspective that can bind them to the feelings of animals, just as deeply as they are alienated from the vertiginous emotional mysteries of dissembling and verbalizing humans. Observing her in his famous account of Grandin, *An Anthropologist on Mars*, neurologist Oliver Sacks noted, "Her sense of animal's moods and feelings is so strong that these almost take possession of her, overwhelm her at times."

Autists *do* get overwhelmed by their feelings. When an autistic child struggles against the crashing sensory wave of human contact, he is not behaving at all strangely, Grandin explains: he is behaving exactly the way a spooked horse might. She would know. Grandin's uncanny autistic ability at both visualizing design and analyzing an animal's perspective, that cow's-eye view, has turned her into the world's foremost designer of meat-processing plants. Early on she witnessed one Iowa slaughterhouse straight out of a Hieronymous Bosch painting, where football-helmeted workers armed with electric prods and nose tongs sent terrified cattle writhing down chutes to horrific deaths. "If hell exists," she wrote in her diary afterward, "I am in it."

Grandin's designs have been undeviating in their focus on removing pain and fear for these animals, and the most extraordinary paean to her slaughterhouse work comes from the utterly unlikely source of Ingrid Newkirk, founder of People for the Ethical Treatment of Animals. "Temple Grandin has done more to reduce suffering in the world than any other person who has ever lived," she recently told *The New Yorker*. Newkirk may have a point. Grandin has eased the lives of untold millions of animals. But have the animals also eased hers?

The dogs are just out there, both of them, loping around and cavorting in the middle of the intersection: An eighteen-wheeler flashes past one, and a Volkswagen Beetle has to slow down and inch past another. They are both Irish setters, running loose in the traffic, and they are having a blast.

"What the . . . What are they doing?" Sergeant McGovern asks me, and shakes his head. "Can you believe this? I can't believe this."

We already have a dog in the car, Billy, a golden Lab who is sticking his snout in and around my ear, vying for a better view of his lucky, lucky friends who are getting to play in traffic. SUVs are barreling by them with AMERICA'S DAIRYLAND license plates, and it's no idle boast, because these dogs are about to get creamed.

"We better do something," his wife, Barb, warns from the backseat.

"Yeah. I guess I . . . I don't know." But he does know. Sergeant McGovern pulls the car off onto the shoulder and gets out. I shrug and follow. I have no idea what we're doing. I started the morning by detouring from a book signing to come here; so now, somehow, I'm arguing with a dog in Wisconsin.

"Here, boy!" McGovern whistles. One dog immediately comes running to him, and the sergeant scoops his hand into the dog's collar, holding him tight.

So I give it a try.

"C'mere! Here, boy! Come on!" I slap my thighs and call to the second dog.

He stands in the median and pounces down on his front legs, wagging his tail—a game! We're playing a game!

"No, come here," I yell, and whistle "I'm not playing. Come on now."

And then, to my amazement . . . he does.

He trots over, neatly missing an RV, and I grab his leather collar. His fur is soaking wet: he and his friend must have been playing in the culvert over by the side of the road. Clinking on his collar is a metal tag: REBEL. Underneath is a Green Bay phone number. I look over at Sergeant McGovern, and he's already got his cell phone out in his free hand. We compare numbers: both dogs have the same owner.

Billy and Barb watch patiently from inside the car; McGovern shakes his head and awkwardly pockets the cell phone, all the while holding on to his dog.

"Nobody home." He marches his dog across the road to a tidy clapboard house, where a young woman is playing in the front yard with her toddler. They talk a moment, and she points at her backyard. Sergeant McGovern turns to me, waves me over, and follows her—and then, so do I. My dog keeps stopping to lick my hand.

"They'll be safe in here," he says when I get there. We are putting the setters in her garage. Her boy stares with frank interest at the dogs, back at his mother, and then at the two entirely random men who have come into his yard.

"My wife can come back and pick them up in a little bit, maybe a half hour," McGovern tells her. "I don't have space in my car right now. I'll leave a message for the owner, too, so they know what's up."

We get back into his gold Saturn sedan. Billy is going berserk sniffing the other dogs on me: I've known Sergeant Thom McGovern for about fifteen minutes, and I already smell like a wet pooch. The county line road stretches before us, and I start wondering how far we are from the prison.

The Sanger Correctional Facility is a squat one-story structure of brown brick; add some monkey bars outside and paint some hopscotch squares, and you'd think it was an elementary school from the 1970s. And it *is* my old elementary school inside: the linoleum, the painted cinder block, the smell of cleanser. There's even a superintendent's office—no one answers to the title of warden here—and above it all, the buzz of institutional fluorescent lighting.

Ribs are being served in the cafeteria; prisoners line up with their trays, and we walk the entire gauntlet. I'm the only visitor here, and every single prisoner in line stares blankly at me: I look down. McGovern doesn't notice—he's used to it. Inmates sitting at tables pause from their lunches to greet the dog with us.

"Billy, hey! Billy-billy-billy!"

"Guys." McGovern nods to them.

When we get to the prison yard out back, a few inmates are languidly bouncing a basketball back and forth, enjoying the first good weather in days.

"Hey," McGovern greets them, and shields his eyes against the sun. "Planning your escape?"

"Naw." They laugh bashfully and tousle Billy. "Man's fooling with us. *Fooling*."

And McGovern is at ease around them. He's here off the clock today; two guards are already at their post in the hub of the wheel-spoke prison, a plexiglassed office that looks down the two cell-block wings and out into the cafeteria. Sergeant McGovern pauses to scratch Billy's head as we walk away, and he nods over at the guard station.

"That's what I did for years before getting this dog program. Just sitting there, all day, like a scarecrow."

I watch them: they watch me back. The clock inside their station crawls slowly. Sergeant McGovern is on his third decade of forty-plus-hour weeks as a corrections officer. It occurs to me that he has now spent more time in prison than most of his inmates.

We crunch over the gravel parking lot in front of the path that winds down from the prison. There are no guard towers, not even any fences. Out by the road, though, is a much older house—an old farmhouse, by the look of it, wedged between the prison building and the county line road. It's hard to imagine anyone wanting to live there, never mind any realtor being able to sell it. Yet hanging out of one of its windows is a guy repainting an old window frame while Foghat hammers away from a little transistor radio.

"That's Independence House," Sergeant McGovern says, following my gaze. "Seven inmates living there. It's a privilege earned for good behavior."

My eyebrows go up: it's a *house*. They could just walk away, saunter down the road.

"They don't try leaving," he interrupts my thought. "Here's the thing. The guys we put in there are lifers, guys on twenty-year terms." My confusion is obvious to him now. "You're thinking they'd run, right? No. Lifers know—they get caught, they go to max. They're motivated by that. Lifers are the reliable ones."

He gestures around. "There's no fences here. This prison was built twenty years ago for sixty prisoners. It's got a hundred and twenty now. Know how many guards? Twelve, total. Two in there at any one time. Two guards, one hundred and twenty prisoners. And we don't have problems, really. Not many incidents. If they screw up here . . . if they can't even handle this, they can wind up in max. And they don't want that. So they stay."

The only fences they need here are for the dogs.

"I guess it's a prison of the mind," he muses.

LIBERTY DOG PROGRAM, the mural announces from the side of the cinder-block building.

"We've got twelve dogs out back. And inside here we're putting in a little living room, just like home," Sergeant McGovern says as he takes me indoors. He gestures at an empty expanse of concrete floor. "It'll have a rug, chairs, sofa, lamps—just all the stuff you'd have in a living room. That way both the dogs and disabled people we're matching them with can train in a realistic setting."

Billy trots around on the concrete as if to emphasize the point.

"Watch this," McGovern says. "Billy? Billy! Get me a beer."

Billy bounds to an old refrigerator pushed over into a corner. The fridge has a thick nautical rope tied around its handle, and Billy takes the rope in his mouth and yanks open the door. Then he reaches in, tilts his jaws around a beer can, and delivers it into McGovern's hands.

"Check out the brand," the sergeant says, and I look at the

practice can. It's gone through a lot and has plenty of scratches and dents from canine teeth, but I can clearly make out its ancient label: BILLY BEER.

"Seemed appropriate." He grins. "Hey, Billy, close the door. You're letting all the cold out. Close the door, Billy."

The dog noses the fridge door shut and waits patiently for his next instruction. He wags in recognition when a trainer walks in.

"Hey, Wally." Sergeant McGovern nods. "Wally'll show you around the kennel. He knows all about the work getting done on this place."

"We've been rebuilding this whole facility, piece by piece," Wally says as he shakes my hand. He's the old-timer here, a guy in his late forties with a voice sanded down by tobacco. He leads me through each room of the cinder-block building. "There's the sergeant's office, bathroom. Storage area up there. Kitchen and laundry."

We pass a rack of doggie vests hanging up on pegs, all marked LIBERTY DOG PROGRAM/SERVICE DOG. Wally pushes open a door into a barnlike area, with smooth concrete floors fragrant with bleach and urine. "And this, this is the kennel. But we take 'em out here to do their business."

We walk outside onto a fenced-in concrete pad.

"Latrine for the dogs," he explains, pointing at the guttered indentations running through the concrete. "Easy to hose down."

On cue, a burly guy walks up and starts hosing it down. He pauses for us to step aside, but not for long. He doesn't look like a guy you keep waiting. As he passes us, I notice a devil's tail tattoo curling out from his shirt collar and up the back of his neck.

"That's Earl," Wally says, lighting another cigarette to replace the one that he has just finished.

Out in the exercise yard, all the dogs are romping around and jumping and wagging and sniffing. "There's Vandy, Rex, Kramer,

Seymour . . ." I lose track of their names immediately; they're all running and whirling around, so it's impossible to keep them straight. A lank prisoner is watching over them, bemused, his arms crossed.

"There's Whit, over there," Wally notes. It takes a moment for me to figure out that he means the man, not one of the dogs. "Anyway, I wish you could have seen how this was. There used to be a twenty-foot drop here. We filled it in so the dogs'd have a place to run. It's all changed over the last year. Lots of guys putting in a lot of work. Everything was donated—the fill, those trees there, the grass. We did a lot of work, though. And that over there"—he points at a small observation post over a training ground—"I'm looking forward to working on that, since I'm a carpenter."

I nod. Growing up, I actually had a contractor neighbor who built prisons. He eventually wound up as an inmate in one.

"Compared to other building jobs, wh—" I start to ask, when I notice: If he's a carpenter, why doesn't he have a visitors badge or something? Wally doesn't have a guard badge hanging from his belt like Sergeant McGovern, either. Or . . . anything.

It dawns on me: he's a prisoner, too.

"Wally's in for vehicular manslaughter," Sergeant McGovern says as his wife finds a videotape from the office bookshelf. "He's not even from here, you know that? He's a carpenter from Florida. He was just up visiting. Had a crash, and a woman died. He's been here five years now. Good guy who made a bad decision."

I look out the window a moment. It's all sort of surreal: that you could go on a trip to see some friends and in one moment never make it home—to suddenly turn from a free man to a prisoner.

"He has a kid who was born right after he came here, and he's barely seen that kid," McGovern adds. "It's hard on him. But that's prison. It's hard on officers, too. They retire at fifty, and they're dead at fifty-five. I'm serious. The jobs eats you up inside. All that negativity. I mean, I worked in a max facility before this. The worst. It was just the worst. And you just think, you know, I don't want my job to be about . . . There has to be something more. Some point to it."

Music wells up from the video. There's prisoners training the dogs; a prisoner-made doggie float for the local Thanksgiving parade; prisoners and disabled owners and hundreds of onlookers for the dog graduation, when they finish their training. It is miraculous that it happens at all. The Liberty Dog program started years ago, and it has nearly died every one of those years. Politicians don't like it much, because nobody likes prisoners very much—not even prisoners who train dogs for the disabled. Everybody loves to be tough on crime; it's much tougher to know what to *do* with your criminals. No one wins votes for thinking hard about that. Yet the idea seems like a wonderfully obvious one. We need prisons; we need guide dogs. It takes time and an exercise yard to train guide dogs, and prisoners have nothing but time and an exercise yard.

"There's so many misconceptions . . ." The sergeant pauses. He searches for the right words. "The guys in prison, don't get me wrong about them. They belong there. They're here for a reason. But that can't be the end of the story. People don't understand why inmates care about training these dogs for disabled kids, why they're proud of their work. Because . . . see, nobody wants to know about the inmates. They want to forget them, not have to think about them. And, well, the disabled . . . I think inmates get it."

"They get what?"

"They get being pushed aside. They get people ignoring them."

It makes sense; the fate of any one is unnervingly replicated in the pain of others. "Capital punishment states are the worst animal states," Temple Grandin once noted, "and the worst for the handicapped."

McGovern reaches over his computer and clicks at photo files.

"I don't know if what we're doing will work. But I know what doesn't work, because I've seen it. I've been there." He taps the monitor. "Hey, take a look at these."

The photo files open up: children with MS, cerebral palsy, spinal injuries, all the crippling ills the young body is prone to. They are sitting with their dogs, smiling.

"Here's a girl whose car rolled over. She's in a wheelchair, and there was a death in her family, too, separate from that. Popular girl at the high school, and suddenly all this happens to her. Just breaks your heart. And when I saw the picture of her with her dog . . . man, it choked me up. That was it."

He clicks on a photo of a ten-year-old boy lying on a bed, gazing and smiling at a dog lying next to him.

"That's Liam. He's autistic."

An entire autistic high school, the Orion Academy, has been created in California based in part around the use of these "service dogs"—to create companionship for the students, but also to cultivate their empathetic relation to humans. But you don't need a specially trained dog for that: all dogs, aside maybe from pit bulls, already make pretty good friends. So I think instead of the usual things service dogs do: pulling open fridge doors, retrieving things, leading a person around. None of them seem to fit for this.

"What do you train for with autism?"

"Danger. Spotting danger. That's the first thing. Autistic kids might try running into a pool of water, or into the street—you know, they see something and they're interested in it, they focus on it, and they don't notice anything else. The parents worry about that. So basically the dogs help shepherd them. And also, the dog's a connection to other people. It's their interpreter. That's true with all the people we work with, but you can really see it with someone like Liam."

If autistics are the ultimate introverts, dogs are the ultimate extroverts. They are all about pack behavior, about being social: they are constantly noticing the world around them. Dogs don't read, they don't take apart pianos when you're not looking, they don't reprogram your computer. But they're very good at seeing when someone is trying to be friendly to you or when someone is threatening you: exactly the things an autist misses. The two are made for each other.

I try to imagine what this place must look like to McGovern's autistic visitors. But here's what you don't see at Sanger Correctional Facility: *inmates* who are autistic. You don't see them much in any prison. Autists tend to keep out of trouble by keeping to themselves. It's hard to be antisocial if you don't notice society in the first place.

"We're training Liam and that dog for graduation next summer," McGovern says. "The look he gets on his face when he has him . . . Well, I mean, just look at it."

I nod and look more closely at the photo: it's an expression I've seen before. It's the look Morgan had with his Big Bird doll. He has a friend.

CHAPTER 15

The letter magnets on the fridge keep getting arranged into words. But not English words. *Bromed. Thwop. Droush. Kiw. Wepding.* They look like words; they sound like them. They have the form of words. And yet . . .

Morgan seizes my arm, pulls me over to the microwave, and pushes my hand to a bag of popcorn kernels.

"What do you want, Morgan?"

"What-you-want-mo-gan."

"What do you want? Tell Daddy."

"Tell-Daddy."

"Use your words. *Your* words. What is this?" I point.

He won't.

"Morgan? . . . Morgan, look at me, honey. Look at Daddy."

He stares intensely into the middle distance.

"Morgan? Look at Daddy. *Look* at Daddy. Look. At. Daddy. Can you say 'popcorn'? Popcorn. Can you say 'popcorn' for Daddy?"

I gently hold his chin in my hand and try to guide his face around. His face is now pointed squarely at mine, but his eyes still avoid me. He *can* look at me. He does it all the time. Sometimes he will suddenly look up at me, full in the eye, and guide my finger to a word that he needs help with. Sometimes it's because he wants me to pick him up, to cuddle and sing to him. Sometimes he'll stop what he is doing to simply smile or look plainly at me: *You are Daddy. I am with you.*

But not right now.

"Morgan, can you sa—"

"*Popco*," he whispers.

He says it without looking at me. But he says it.

Words come sifting out. Ice cream. TV. Outside. One day Marc calls us from the playground, almost too excited to talk. "He said my name. He said my name! He was stuck on the jungle gym and needed help, and he said '*Marc*'!" The words come out one by one, slowly. There are no sentences, no phrases even at first, just words: but words matched to things that he wants. Barb's classes at school and endless card drills with him at home are inching him forward, slowly but noticeably. A few words he says all the time; others he'll say once and discard. There are some we can't figure out at all and a few we hope he doesn't figure out, either.

We sprawl on the big bed, me with a newspaper, Morgan slumped across my feet and turning pages in a book. The book is a comically immense compilation of twentieth-century news stories—one of those oversized and overpriced hardcover slabs that got remaindered as soon as everyone stopped giving a damn about the new millennium. It's the biggest book on our bedroom bookshelf, and Morgan has lately taken to reaching for it first thing in the morning, crashing it like a boulder from the bookshelf to the floor, heaving it from the floor onto the bed, and then methodically leafing through its 1,500 pages. One morning I woke to the sound of him announcing the headlines from December 1919, like a radio announcer reading the incoming wires. "Senate

Votes Against Ver-sa-lies Treaty." Pause. "New Law Reduces Child Labor . . ."

But on this afternoon he is reading the book silently, stopping occasionally to press his face against the cool glossy paper of the color plates. Suddenly he clambers over my newspaper, slaps away the National section, and grabs my fingers.

"What do you want, little guy?"

"Want you want," he echoes.

He pulls my hand over to a line in the book: he wants me to read a headline from July 1921.

"Okay, then." I examine it. *"De Valera in London to Begin Peace Talks."*

He jabs my finger at one word.

"Valera. Valera," I say. "Valeravaleravalera. Oh . . . you want to know what it means. I . . . uh, hmm."

He waits patiently.

"Valera is a *man*," I say. "A man whose name is Valera."

I hold my breath, waiting for him to jam my finger into the word again, unsatisfied with my circular logic. I see him looking at the next headline over—TWO ITALIAN ANARCHISTS CONVICTED OF MUR-DER—this is worse. I don't want to explain any word in it, other than *two* and *of*. And I'm not even sure how to define *of*. But he tosses my hand away; I'm dismissed.

The entire outside world, starting with people simply saying "Hello," remains so alien that I wouldn't know how to start with these other things. How would you explain war? Or peace, which would necessitate explaining war? Or Italians or Irish, which means explaining countries, which in turn means explaining war again? Or murder, which in turn probably means explaining that people may have ill intentions toward one another, which . . . well, back to war again, really. And behind it all, working the controls, is death. Life does not make much sense to him yet; how could death?

When the philosopher Hippolyte Taine observed a toddler in 1876, he marveled: "Her first question is always: 'What does it say? What does the rabbit say? What does the bird say? What does the horse say? What does the big tree say?' Whether it be an animal or a tree, she treats the object as a person; wants to know what it thinks, what it says." Everything in the world seemed alive to Taine's toddler, and likewise nothing really seemed dead:

> When this child's doll had its head broken she was told that now the doll was dead. One day her grandmother said to her: "I am old, I shall not be long with you; I shall die." "Your head will be broken, then." This she repeated several times. Even yet (age, three years and one month), to be dead means, for her, to have a broken head. The day before yesterday a magpie that had been killed by a gardener was tied to the top of a pole for a scarecrow; on being told that the pie was dead the child wished to see it. "What does the pie do," she asked. "She does nothing; she will never stir again, she is dead." "Oh!" For the first time the idea of final immobility has entered her mind. Now let us suppose a people to stop at this idea, and to have no other definition of death than this. For them the Beyond will be the Sheol of the Hebrews—the place where the motionless dead live a vague sort of life.

There are no dead magpies hanging in our garden. And whenever a violent movie trailer appears on TV we dive to shut it off. Morgan has never seen a gun; never seen a picture of a gun: he does not know that there could be such a thing as a gun. Violence, death, countries, criminals, guns, wars—they are not merely hard to explain to him. We haven't even ventured there. The concepts do not exist yet.

Jennifer gets home from taking him to school, shrugs off her jacket, and kicks her shoes away with a sigh of relief.

"Walked back?"

She nods. We don't have a car; Morgan gets to school by taxi, and Jennifer returns by bus or, when the weather's nice, she likes to walk the fifty blocks home.

"These new shoes are not for walking in," she tells me.

"That's a pretty damning indictment for a shoe."

"Well, they're not for walking fifty blocks in, at least." She rummages through her coat for a folded-up sheet of paper. "I saw a house for sale on the way back, by Mount Tabor."

She passes me the real estate flyer: a prewar Tudor with mod cons, ugly siding that needs ripping away, a big grassy yard.

"Hmm."

Jennifer and I eye other people's home listings out of sheer voyeurism. We already have a home to live in, a nice home. I love that our house has century-old floorboards that creak with every step and the rambling feel of a building that has been shaped and reshaped every couple of decades on the whim of generations of previous owners. It's house you can live on one floor of without going upstairs for anything—which also makes it a house you could grow old in. And I would be happy to never move again.

Still . . .

"This place in the listing is a duplex."

"Yeah, I noticed that."

"If we ever did move . . . sometimes I think that would be the way to go."

"If one of our parents ever needs to live with us, it makes sense."

"Right."

"And Morgan, when he's older . . ."

"Yeah. Yeah."

"Or a place with guest house, a live-in garage out back. That'd work."

"That might be better. Give him more privacy, but we'd still . . . you know. We'd still be there."

We listen to the birds through our living room window, thinking ahead twenty, thirty, forty years. I look at the two pictures on our piano: one is of Jennifer and me, taken when we eloped to a park in British Columbia, nothing but us and the local justice of the peace, her assistant, and some quacking ducks to witness. A pair of toddlers with bags of stale bread ran giggling through the middle of our vows, which seemed appropriate. The other picture is a couple of years later on a San Francisco street; it's me holding Morgan at six months. His face gazes straight into the camera, though perhaps he was really looking at the N-Judah train rolling by behind us.

I guess I already knew then that all parenting is lifelong, or should be. But now it's different. I think of an autism specialist I spoke to recently; when our conversation turned to what happened to autists in adulthood, I breezily pointed at a case where a forty-year-old autist, a traffic-flow engineer, was still living with his parents.

"I suppose there's always that possibility that an autist will live with or next door to their family for the rest of their lives," I said.

The specialist raised his eyebrows at my choice of words. "It's not a *possibility*," he corrected me. "It's a *probability*."

This should be a shock. Yet it isn't. It should be hard to get my mind around, I guess . . . but, no. Not letting go of your child is the easiest thing in the world to understand.

And we probably can't. Even when they learn productivity and independence and—well, all those fine qualities that you're supposed to be instilling in them—autists do not recognize half of what is happening around them. They can be taken advantage of, they can neglect themselves, they can vanish and no one will know. You cannot just send them out into the world like that. So generations live together in the house, or next door to each other, just as they used to. The talented but awkward adult autist is your classic geek who still lives in his parents' house. What's odd is that, in our mobile society, this ancient arrangement now seems like an aberration.

I'm in my office, leafing through a book I recently found, Ellery Walter's 1928 autobiography, *The World on One Leg*. Yes, it is precisely what its title promises. I'm at the chapter set in Fiji. After being denounced as a "one-legged devil," our hero and his sidekick hear something whistle past them while they eat dinner in his hut: "By the flickering flame, we saw a long cruel knife deeply embedded in the matted wall."

Then *I* start hearing something whistling. *Eeeet. Tweeeeet. Eee-eee-eeee.* It is coming from downstairs. When I reach the living room, I find Jennifer and Marc smiling and watching Morgan as he stands in front of the TV, where he is blowing manically on a little wooden recorder. He is keeping time with . . . with . . .

I turn to Jennifer.

"Are you *trying* to warp our child?"

It is Lawrence Welk.

"Oh, honey. He *loves* it. Look at him."

It's true. And the Lawrence Welk orchestra is, well, not jamming exactly, but—you know, actually, there's this woman doing an accordion solo, and I have to admit that she's rocking out.

"Wow," Marc says. "They need a mosh pit."

Morgan is ignoring all of us and presses his face up to the TV screen to get the full Welk-surround experience. He is fascinated by the orchestra, especially when the tubas and trumpets kick in. Even before he could walk, he was transfixed by radio ads featuring saxophones. He now has a colliery brass band album that he loves: he will put it on and just sit in front of the stereo with the speakers framing his head, basking in the sound as though it's the warm glow of a sun lamp.

The camera pulls out to show the whole Welk orchestra, revealing over them the giant sign of the show's sponsor: GERITOL. We all burst out laughing—except for Morgan. He's still dancing. And why not? There are no uncool interests to Morgan, no peer pressure, because there are no peers. There are other autistic kids who like watching Laurel and Hardy or golf games, or listening to Bach incessantly. If they like something, they like it: they don't really care what you think.

A tap dancer comes out, clicking away to the accompaniment of the orchestra. Morgan gleefully jackhammers his feet against the floor, and then he sort of moonwalk shuffles a few steps backward. He is delighted.

"We should tape this stuff for him," Jennifer says.

"Yeah." I nod. "Sure. Let's start taping Lawrence Welk."

So we've volunteered to get the drinks for the children's party that will close the last day of school; after we drop Morgan off in Barb's classroom, Jennifer and I trudge out to the grubby motelish strip ten blocks away. There are two supermarkets along this strip of Eighty-second Avenue; the first doesn't look too promising. For one thing, its parking lot is empty. Also, it has a cyclone fence around it.

"I don't think we'll find our apple juice here," Jennifer says.

"No." I sigh, then brighten up. "Maybe we'll find a body!"

We creep up to the storefront and peer in through the windows. It's big and empty inside, with wires hanging down where light fixtures and false ceilings used to be, worn floors of dirty linoleum with jagged little metal stubs sticking up where the shelving was torn out. Against the walls, a few of the old department signs are visible in the semidarkness: MEATS & DELI, BAKERY, FISH. The signs and walls have the avocado green and sunny orange of a me-decade grand opening; a generation has come and gone and left this neighborhood behind, and now so has their old supermarket. The tattered notice in the window shows it was closed months ago.

"There's another place a few blocks down," she says. "I'm sure they'll have whatever we need."

Only it sort of doesn't. The other store is full of weird off-brands, the stuff that gets pawned off on inner-city bodegas and new immigrants.

"What the hell?" I hoist up a gallon jug. *"Purity Splash?"*

"Hygiene product?"

"Orange drink," I read from the label. "Oh dear."

The aisles are full of Russian and Vietnamese food; they are the new face of this neighborhood, even though you don't see their kids in the special ed classes . . . yet. In a new country without health coverage, their children won't be diagnosed until it's terribly late, until long after they've started elementary school. Second-language difficulties might hide such things for years more.

I regard the sickly orange drink and stare down the aisles. We are very lucky.

*　　*　　*

"Hi, Morgan! . . . Morgan? Morgan, hi!"

Morgan looks up when we enter the classroom with our grocery bag full of juice boxes; other parents are arriving with cupcakes and cookies. We joined late in the school year, and now all of a sudden it's coming to a close. But for these kids the school year doesn't really end. You can't leave them out for months at a time. They'll be back in a few weeks, some channeled into specialist classes by disorder, others into more general age-specific classes. Dylan, his panic attacks largely gone now, won't be back at all; he's made it into the mainstream preschool. Perhaps he is the exception. Some kids in the building aren't mainstream, and they're not in tributaries, either. They are swimming in their own oceans.

"Hi, Morgan!" Jennifer repeats again.

Barb gently holds Morgan's hand and works it through a waving motion.

"Hi," she prompts him.

"Hi," he says offhandedly, looking away while giving us a small wave.

They have been working on "Hi" and "Come here" for a couple of months now: the crucial first steps to interaction. He's starting to get it, though it takes hundreds of run-throughs to learn social routines the rest of us take for granted. Morgan leans against me and then Jennifer, smiling faintly, pressing warmly against us. This is his way of saying hi, regardless of the rest of the world's custom.

"Hey, Morgan," I point. "Who's that? Who's that over there?"

"Barb," he whispers.

"Good job!" Jennifer says. Now she points at one of the assistants. "Who's that? Morgan, who's that?"

He wanders away.

"Try again." She leads him back and turns his head toward the teacher working with Kwame on the other side of the classroom.

"Who's that?" She points.

"Bruce," he mutters.

"Good job! Now . . ." She turns Morgan toward me. "Who's that?"

Morgan smiles and looks away.

"I see you there." I tickle him, and he cracks up.

"Look up, Morgan," Jennifer coaxes him. "Who's that?"

He won't say. He just won't do it. He has never addressed either of us by name.

We decide to make examples of each other.

"Hi, Daddy!" Jennifer waves broadly to me.

"Hi, Mommy!" I wave back cheerfully.

Morgan regards this little skit indifferently and then walks away to the toy box. He holds up a little drum and presses his nose against the clear drumhead. Its circumference frames his face like the old-fashioned helmet of a deep-sea diver, staring at the world through the crushing weight of water.

CHAPTER 16

They are in their own world, sealed within boxes of glass and wood: compartmentalized constructions of stuffed birds, scraps of *Baedeker* maps, assemblages of children's marbles and disembodied doll parts, hotel ads and pharmacy jars. Their construction is somewhere between that of a curio cabinet and a Japanese bento box; alternating historical engravings and fragments of forgotten books sit side by side with the mundane debris of everyday life. Each piece on its own is curiously interesting but gives no clue to any greater meaning; but then, when you stand back and see the box assembled as a whole, the combination becomes unsettling and beautiful.

The maker of these boxes, Joseph Cornell, had allegedly memorized the contents of junk dealers throughout Manhattan, and it was years before he revealed his purpose. In 1931, Cornell was a stranger lingering awkwardly at closing time in the Manhattan art gallery of Julien Levy. The dealer was busy unpacking surrealist work for an exhibition titled *Newer SuperRealism*; Levy later recalled what happened next:

> "Closing time," I suggested. But he had already fumbled out of his overcoat pocket two or three cardboards on which were painted cutouts of steel engravings. Collages! I glanced hastily at the bundle of

collages by Max Ernst only just unpacked and stacked on the bookshelf. But these were not any of those. "Where did you find these?" . . . "I make them," Joseph said . . .

Soon Levy was featuring Cornell in a paired exhibition alongside Pablo Picasso. Yet his young protégé seemed uninterested in fame or jumping aboard any artistic movement. Critics called Cornell a surrealist, a label he shrugged off. He probably preferred John Ashberry's later description of his work as "a new kind of realism"—for Cornell had always insisted that his work was "down-to-earth." And indeed it was. He would pick things up off the ground, or the most ordinary household objects, and examine them for their intrinsic worth in form and color, rather than what anyone thought they were worth in their original incarnations. Returning from walks through the city, he wrote, "I thought, everything can be used in a lifetime, can't it?"

Cornell loved the dazzling cultural overload of Times Square, and amid the gaudy lights and hawkers he would pick up postcards, photo-booth scraps, and cheap necklaces from Woolworth's; then, moving on to the bookshops of Fourth Avenue, he'd hoard yellowing prints, books, and maps. All this cultural flotsam was packed into the labeled bins he kept at home, awaiting the right wooden case to arrange them into some sense of order. His resulting compartment boxes, which so often include map fragments, turn out to be rather like maps themselves: a way to make sense of the nearly senseless, through gridded-out pictures of a world that is otherwise impossible to take in all at once.

Nobody quite knew what to make of Cornell. He lived outside the art scene, spending his days in a little house on Utopia Parkway in Queens with his mother and his invalid brother, Robert. They rarely had visitors there, freeing Joseph and Robert to build an intricate toy railroad system in their living room. Today his work is sometimes classified as outsider art, a category typically reserved for known savants and mental patients. Cornell bristled at being labeled an eccentric recluse—yet on the day that he died of heart failure in 1972, he called his sister with second thoughts on a matter that was now, and perhaps always had been, beyond his power to change.

"I wish," he mused to her, "I had not been so reserved."

Even as Cornell spoke, a landlord halfway across the country was combing through the abandoned worldly effects and debris left by another deeply reserved old man—one whose life would prove to be even more solitary, complex, and bewildering.

I place my face near the glass: an illustration for *In the Realms of the Unreal*, the curatorial note reads. The pictures are of naked hermaphrodites in a vast panoramic landscape, sketched from magazine illustrations redolent of the Campbell's Soup Kids era of illustration and hand colored; it resides in a gently lit humidity-controlled museum case. I step back and look around the building, at the visitors strolling by. I'm just another bleary out-of-towner myself, on my way to the reading room of the public library, but I can't help thinking about this case being in this *place*. It took a certain contrarian sense of humor to build the American Museum of Folk Art out of cold marble and metal and glass and then plop it down in midtown Manhattan.

The contents of the case—an immense double-sided illustration, a collage, a page of handwritten meteorological jottings—seem an unimaginably long way from their origins in an abandoned apartment at 851 Webster Street in Chicago. It was there, one day in December of 1972, that painter Nathan Lerner trudged upstairs in the tenement building he owned to sort through and empty out the apartment of a retired hospital janitor who had just entered the nursing home.

Inside the apartment of Henry Darger, there was a permanent gloom: a peeling papered ceiling and dark wooden walls enclosing immense piles of yellowing newspapers and magazines, boxes of rubber bands, old shoes, cockeyed appliances and furniture accumulated over the course of sixty years. The shelves and niches were crowded with Catholic ornaments; and then, amid it all, there was art. *Vast* expanses of art. Darger's tables were covered in crayons, paints, glues, scissors, pencils, and endless sheaves of collages. Searching through some old trunks, Lerner discovered dozens of mysterious volumes. The first find, hand-bound in fifteen volumes by Darger, was an epic novel: *In the Realms of the Unreal*. Written on Darger's old manual typewriter, it is a staggering 15,145 pages long—the longest work of fiction in human history. A further three volumes contained hundreds of immense drawings to illustrate the book; some fold out to a full twelve feet in length. And alongside these discoveries, Lerner excavated yet another work: *The History of My Life*. Darger's autobiography is a succinct 5,084 handwritten pages.

No one had any idea this had been going on.

"I did not know Henry for twenty years," his landlord later marveled. "I don't think anyone knew Henry."

In the years after Darger's death in 1973, residents of his building were haunted by the enigma of the upstairs neighbor they almost never saw, an old man whom they tried to look out for—bathing him occasionally and even throwing a birthday party for him—but who seemed curiously unknowable. But Darger himself was also haunted by someone he didn't know. "I lost my sister by adoption," he wrote in *The History of My Life*. "I never knew or seen her, or knew her name." It was an absence that always troubled him. The younger sister had been given up in the wake of Mrs. Darger's death in 1894, when Henry was only three years old, and as the firstborn son he was left to be raised by his hapless father. Young Henry read history and geography voraciously but scarcely understood how to relate to other human beings. He was overwhelmed by his senses at times—particularly by changes in weather, to which he was acutely sensitive. His odd vocalizations and physical tics caused his classmates to award him the nickname "Crazy," which deeply pained the boy.

His loneliness was increased immeasurably when, at the age of twelve, he was placed into the Lincoln Asylum for Feeble Minded Children. Had he not escaped five years later, Darger might have spent the rest of his life there, as many people with autism did. When one decrepit mental hospital was shut down in 1980, and its lifelong residents given exit exams, it was found that 339 of 893 residents had autistic disorders. Almost none had ever been diagnosed, and many had started their lifetime stay in the asylum before the concept of autism had even existed.

Somehow the teenage Darger managed to eke out an existence among the tenements of Chicago. His strangeness was so obvious that after being called up for the draft in 1917, he was immediately rejected by the military. Instead, he spent decades as a janitor at local hospitals, a patient who'd escaped cleaning up after the ones who hadn't. He lived quite alone, though he longed for a dog, and apparently had notions of adopting a child, too—something he was as unlikely to get as a military commission. Darger ardently wished he were a child again himself; adults did not make sense and had never done much but hurt him. He went to church and pondered why the God that he had been raised under seemed so arbitrarily cruel as well.

At home, after his long hours of janitorial work, Darger poured out an imaginary world where he was a hero saving imperiled children. *In the Realms of the Unreal* is an epic about a revolt by child slaves, occurring on a planet a thousand times the size of the earth and populated by trillions of inhabitants. Darger began writing it in 1911, just a couple of years after his escape from the asylum, and continued until 1971, when he was too weak to continue. *Realms* is a shutting out of the outside world, the literary equivalent of living inside Darger's head: "At a certain point the length of a written work can change its nature completely," notes his biographer, John MacGregor. "It ceases to be a book, or a piece of writing to be read . . . [and becomes] a means of living for a lifetime in another world."

But it is a deeply unsettling world, one of endless slaughter and misery—and those who would control this world must first control the weather. The Realm is constantly beset by floods, tornadoes, tidal waves, and blizzards; millions of people at a time die in immense meteorological cataclysms that rage across the landscape. The hero of the book is one Hendro Darger—a meteorologist.

What is so maddening about the weather is that, like God Himself, it is omnipresent, uncontrollable, and unpredictable. These were the most frightening qualities imaginable to Darger. When he began his epic, meteorologists were still making the shakiest of weather predictions based on barometer readings telegraphed in from around the country—a system pioneered by Admiral Robert FitzRoy. If FitzRoy is remembered at all today, it is as Charles Darwin's rather strange captain on HMS *Beagle*. The two men shared a cabin together for five years and drove each other very nearly insane in the process. Darwin found the moody and curiously distant captain a complete enigma—it wasn't even until after the voyage that he discovered that FitzRoy, his roommate for five years, had been engaged all along to be married. But then, FitzRoy came from a famously eccentric family and had stepped into a job clearly perilous to one's sanity; the previous captain of the *Beagle* had blown his brains out. FitzRoy did not fare much better after his voyages. After using barometer readings and new telegraph technology to invent weather forecasting, FitzRoy was so distraught by its spotty results— and by merciless ridicule in the London papers—that he slit his own throat. Today we take blaming the weatherman for granted, but the true extent of the roiling chaos of meteorological phenomena was something that neither FitzRoy nor London columnists of the day could have realized.

"I always hated the second law of thermodynamics," Temple Grandin once noted. Entropy is anathema to the autistic; the world is already intolerably chaotic, and it should not be permitted to get worse. Still, to try to apply order to weather would seem the height of hopelessness. But stepping into FitzRoy's shoes decades later was the meteorologist Lewis Fry Richardson—a man who, when asked to describe his hobbies, answered, "Solitude." In 1922, Richardson published his mathematical masterpiece, *Weather Prediction by Numerical Process*. Richardson had taken measurements from across Europe for May 20, 1910, and had spent years working *backward* from the measurements to develop differential equations that could account for the weather patterns over the course of the day. These, in turn, could be used to predict weather in the future.

Richardson concluded his book with a fantastic proposal for an immense and dazzling spherical hall where sixty-four thousand human "computers" could crunch numbers for forecasts:

> The walls of this chamber are painted to form a map of the globe. The ceiling represents the north polar regions, England is in the gallery, the tropics in the upper circle, Australia on the dress circle and the Antarctic in the pit. A myriad of computers are at work upon the weather of the part of the map where each sits . . . A tall pulpit rises to half the height of the hall. In this sits the man in charge . . . He is like a conductor of an orchestra in which the instruments are slide-rules and calculating machines. But instead of waving a baton he turns a beam of rosy light upon any region that is running ahead of the rest, and a beam of blue light upon those who are behindhand.

Richardson was a great believer in numbers: the lonesome meteorologist spent his later years pondering how math could be fruitfully applied to solving problems in psychology and geopolitics. Math, he thought, might prevent wars. It seems a curiously naïve belief, at odds with any realistic sense of how the world works. And it certainly is at odds with any sense of how *we* feel it works. But then, so were George Boole's attempts at resolving all philosophy into mathematical statements—yet that eccentric mathematician's work also proved to have unforeseen uses a century later.

And Richardson? His hopeless scheme for a grand hall of human computers remained dormant for decades until digital computers came along. His calculations, it turns out, are at the bedrock of modern meteorology.

It was impossible for Henry Darger to avoid thinking about the weather for long. In *The History of My Life*, his autobiography takes up only the first 200 pages before getting swept away by a tornado: the next 4,900 pages are spent describing a sentient vortex named Sweetie Pie. Instead of raging against the God that he could not understand, Darger fulminates upon an immense and arbitrary maelstrom that existed only within his own imagination. The endless destructive funnel of Sweetie Pie is eventually put on trial for "unnatural acts," with the heroic meteorologist Darger as a prosecutor.

"Weather," notes biographer John MacGregor, "was his chief, some say his only, topic of conversation."

It was not an interest that one would expect many relationships to be formed upon, and the real Henry Darger was indeed an almost utterly solitary man . . . almost. He did have one friend: a laborer like himself named William Schloeder. On their days off, the two took walks in Lincoln Park, dined together, and generally seemed to understand each other; the only existing photograph of Darger as a young man shows the two together on a local outing. William, who lived with his parents or his sister for his entire life, may well have been the one man whom Darger had everything in common with— a neurological fellow traveler. They remained friends for nearly fifty years until Schloeder's death of old age and flu in 1959.

"I am alone," Darger wrote in his journal after Schloeder's death. "I never palled with anyone since."

Darger did have one project to immerse himself in, though, to try to make some sense of the confusing and unfair world around him. On New Year's Eve of 1957, he had begun to keep a journal titled *Weather Report of Cold and Warm, Also Summer Heats and Cool Spells, Storms, and Fair or Cloudy Days, Contrary to What the Weatherman Says, and True Too.* The title seems straight out of an eighteenth-century almanac, and the journal's contents are exactly as described:

Tuesday Dec 10 1963

Partly sunny and cold today. General cloudiness towards evening. 6
to 8 a.m. 22 degrees, noon till 5 a.m. 28, 29 degrees at 3 pm. West to
northwest winds. 8 p.m. 25 above.

It is a daily record of Chicago's weather, sometimes echolalically
copying the exact utterance of newspaper weather reports, while at
other times his entries include his own comments on the weather,
plus critiques of the ever-erroneous weathermen. Darger was up at
all hours taking temperature readings, noting the day's high and
low, and comparing it with the weathermen's reports. "Wrong in all
predictions," he characteristically notes of the weathermen on
November 11, 1966.

Darger's art and his vast books are his most famous work today;
his weather journals remain less known and strangely inexplicable.
Yet they were his most sustained effort of his entire life as an artist, a
ten-year commitment that he dedicated part of every day to. His
accumulated journals filled up six ring binders. But then, weather is
measurable, translatable into numbers, even as it is unpredictable in
its manifestations. Darger believed in and struggled against the God
that he had been raised to believe in; the weather, descending from
the heavens, was the one evidence of God's workings that could be
analyzed and compared each day, even by a poor man in a poor
tenement.

His observations ended on New Year's Eve of 1967, ten years
to the day after they started, and conclude with a single word
from Darger's pen: "Finish." He never explained to anyone else
why he did it. The meaning was clear to him, and that was
enough.

*   *   *

"Have you ever painted light bulbs?" The man across the coffee-house is talking too loudly. "Do you know what happens when you paint them orange?"

No, I don't, and I don't particularly want to find out. I hold my newspaper up higher, to shield myself from the conversations in the café, and try to catch up on the local news that I missed while I was out of town. But a couple of sentences into an article I stop reading; I look outside into the Portland traffic, and—what is going on? I quietly lower my paper. It's a crowded coffeehouse, but at the other side of the room a middle-aged man in a windbreaker is addressing a group of what appear to be MBA students: young, smartly attired, one of them using an expensive laptop. They sit and stare around their table, rolling their eyes.

"You don't get the same effect if you paint a light bulb blue," the lecturer earnestly tells the supercilious fellow with the laptop. "Have you tried that—painting light bulbs blue? You don't get blue light. See, you get different color light depending on how you mix the paint. Maybe it depends on the kinds of filament . . ."

The student doesn't answer. In fact, he doesn't even look up at the man addressing him. He just gives a who-is-this-loser smile to the girl next to him. No one there is even looking at the man; they're just waiting for him to go away. But—strange—the man is not really looking at them, either, as he speaks.

"I've tried mixing different paint colors, too," the man rambles on in a monotone. "Sometimes if you add in some violet . . ."

The guy with the laptop sighs loudly to his friends, and they make scoffing sounds, and . . . I just want to shake the bastard, snap his laptop in two, and—*Can't you at least be polite?*—but I just sit and watch helplessly from across the coffeehouse, as the fellow rattles on and on and they still refuse to acknowledge his existence.

And then, suddenly, it's my turn.

"Have you painted light bulbs?" The man is standing in front of me. "Do you know what happens when you paint them orange?"

"Um . . ." I fumble. "No, I guess I haven't tried—"

"You get red. It depends on the kind of paints you use, but you get a light with a lot of red in it. Same with brown. If you paint a light bulb brown, you'll get red and even some green in it."

"Oh. I didn't know that."

"Most people don't know how the colors work, but I figured it out by painting them myself. And . . ."

He barrels on with his account of the varieties of light bulb experience, and I shrink into my chair and let him continue his monologue. I'm stuck there, trapped in a conversation where I'm not even needed, because it's as though he's talking right through and past me. But I don't dare leave; I can't, I just can't go and pretend this man isn't there.

I'm about four blocks away when I sit down on the steps of a church. I'm not religious. It's because if you cry on the steps of a church, no one bugs you. If you cry on a homeowner's front steps, they call the police.

I can't bear the thought that someday, somehow, someone will be cruel to my child. Or pretend that he is not even there.

In the end, it was a Common Grounds employee who extricated me; she'd seen Painted Light Bulb Guy before, obviously, and gently led him away—"Maybe this nice man would like to finish his coffee now," she told him—but I did not finish my coffee, and I did not feel like a nice man. I felt useless. You'd think I'd have some idea by now of how to talk to an autistic person, but I don't. I know how to talk to my son. That's about it. He is slowly figuring out how to talk to us, I guess. He cried out "Mommy" for the first time last week, after skinning his knee on the driveway; we haven't gotten to "Daddy" yet but are trying.

I pluck some blades of grass out of the church's lawn and idly examine them and then toss them. What if you couldn't just look at a lawn like this one? What if you kept seeing all the individual blades, and it overwhelmed you, paralyzed you? What if . . . No, no. I can't be overwhelmed, too. I get up, brush myself off, and start walking home.

You know, it used to be that when I saw someone acting or talking strangely, or just being odd on the bus, I'd think to myself: What's his problem? I still have that reaction. But now I stop, pause, and have a second thought: No, really, what *is* that man's problem? There is a decades-long chain of events that created the person you're seeing. Maybe all you can do is silently wish them godspeed, and try not to be cruel and stupid to them. Maybe you can wonder at how little separates you from them. Then again, maybe a *lot* separates you. And yet—are they so far separated from others who, though odd, are deemed great by the world?

It has become something of a parlor game in the press to wonder aloud at which eccentric geniuses might have been autistic. Newton and Einstein are perennial favorites. Others require little guess-work—the mathematician Paul Erdos, say, or the pianist Glenn Gould, whose uncontrollable vocalizing is embedded within his piano recordings as a musically echolaliac accompaniment to his instrument. And then there is that epitome of postmodern life, Andy Warhol, displaying the curiously familiar combination of discon-nected affect, guileless social observation, and repetitive visual obsessions, all while living with his mother and painstakingly collecting seemingly random items into hundreds of boxes in his apartment. To think that some of our paragons of art and science might be autistic outsiders is to get a shock of recognition. A genius must assiduously ignore others in order to be guided by his own curiosity, by a desire to make sense of the world. And can't the same can be said of the light bulb painter?

There is no way to know what an immense concentration and radically altered perspective will alight upon. To someone with great focus, the fascination is the point. It was blind, brilliant, dumb luck that we had an Isaac Newton who focused on something that other people found important. There are Newtons of refrigerator parts, Newtons of painted light bulbs, Newtons of train schedules, Newtons of bits of string. Isaac Newton happened to be the Newton of Newtonian physics, and you cannot have him without having the others, too.

CHAPTER 17

The stickers are carefully lined up across the living room window: the sun, Mercury, Venus . . . it took me a week until, lying on the floor one day, I looked up and realized what Morgan had done. He'd not only placed the planets into their proper orbits, but he'd picked the one window where, when he sits beneath it, the planets appear suspended in a clear blue sky. I stare at the planets, and at the sunlight streaming onto the couch. Morgan is lying there, quietly sorting through math cards: 2+3=5.

"Morgan?" I hold his hand to my face, to try to draw his gaze to me. Sometimes it works. "Morgan, what do you want to eat?"

He waves me off and continues looking at his cards. There are only a few foods that he'll deign to eat, anyway: others are treated as though they are nonexistent, not even food, as if we'd put a heap of rocks on his plate. We have to sneak things into his diet without him noticing, in much the same way that Jennifer has to cut his hair while he's asleep. If there were a way to feed Morgan spinach while he slept, we'd probably try that, too.

I go into the kitchen to forage for him, and Marc is already there, preparing a travel cup of juice so that he can play with Morgan outside for a while.

"I don't know if I told you," Marc says. "Do you know what he did the other day?"

"What'd he do?"

"Well, we were drawing faces—or, I was, and then he took the pen from me and started drawing them himself." Marc opens the fridge and pulls out a container of apple juice. "So anyway, he's drawing faces for a long time, and then I see him writing letters. And . . . and . . . you know what, I'll draw it for you."

Marc sets down the juice bottle, grabs a scratch pad out of his back pocket, and sketches quickly on it.

"This is what he drew." He passes it to me.

I hold up the drawing and stare at it; then I look at him sprawled on the couch, laying out the math cards into straight lines. The living room is quiet except for the soft hum of the computer, which he's left without bothering to click on the final box—

Are you sure you want to quit?

YES   NO

The cursor arrows waits expectantly within the screen.

How do you get outside of your head? It has to be in a way he can relate to. We have our little cards labeled **popcorn** and **juice** that he sometimes hands us, but we don't really know how to make him talk or respond to a question, exactly—we're just making it all up as we go along, and so is he.

I look at Morgan. Then I look at the computer screen again.

YES   NO

How? How?

"Okay." I lay a pad of paper in front of him. "Morgan, look."

I turn the sheet around to its side, so that the rectangle assumes the shape of a computer screen. Then I write out the words in large letters:

I WANT

a bagel   yogurt

"Morgan," I ask, "what do you want to eat?"

He grabs my finger without hesitation and stabs it at **bagel**.

I can hardly believe it.

"Morgan? Are you sure? Is that what you want?"

He jams my finger down again and again:

Bagel. Bagel. Bagel bagel bagel.

I can't quite believe it works. It inverts the usual way a child develops: instead of learning to speak and transmuting that speech into reading and computing, Morgan's first impulse is computing and reading. Is that how he understands speaking?

"You want a bagel," I say, trying to keep my voice calm.

"Bagel," he repeats.

"Good job! Can you say, 'I want a bagel'?"

"CanyousayIwantabagel."

"Close enough." I hug him.

I go to the kitchen for his bagel, feeling slightly dazed. It is only two sentences: a question and an answer. I'm not sure, but I think my son and I may have just had our first conversation.

In a few days there are piles of questions strewn around the room.

DO YOU WANT TO GO OUTSIDE?

yes   no

I WANT

a peanut butter sandwich   toast with butter

ARE YOU SLEEPY?

yes   no

I WANT TO GO TO THE

library   playground

It doesn't always work. The sketch pad is battered from being thrown across the room in disgust. Sometimes he just doesn't want to know, doesn't get it, doesn't like the choices . . . I don't know. Sometimes he just gets mad and shoves it away. But . . . sometimes he doesn't.

Plink plink.

"Morgan, no!" I rush across the house. He is inside the piano again, grabbing at the hammers. "No, no, honey. That hurts the hammers."

I pry him back, but he just leans back inside, now holding on to my shirt for balance. He thinks I'm here to help aid in his inspection. *Plink*, he starts again.

"Morgan . . ." I haul him back onto the piano bench. "You can play the piano. *Play* the piano. And you can *watch* the hammers. But don't grab them."

We have this action and reaction twenty, thirty times a day. He gets inside the piano, I pull him out again. There is no malice in it, no defiance: he is enraptured by its workings and instantly forgets the two or three thousand times we have pulled him out of the piano before. At that moment, he cannot think of anything else but mashing the keys with his knees and feet while sticking his head inside the piano to observe the hammers, the dampers, the strings, and the pegs.

But our truce works, for the moment, at least, and he decides to play.

"This little pig went to market," he sings as he bangs the keys, "this little pig stayed ho-oooo-me . . ." He turns around on the bench, playing with his hands behind his back. "This little pig had roast beef . . ." He jumps up and mashes out an entire octave with his bottom. *"This little pig had none!"*

"Okay. Morgan . . ."

He walks up and down the keyboard.

"And this little pig went wee wee wee all the waaaaaaaay . . . hooooome."

Then he pops up the lid and grabs the hammers again.

"Morgan, no!" I rush across the room. "No, no, honey . . ."

*　　*　　*

I can't beat it, so I might as well join it.

"Where's the music section?" I ask the Powell's bookstore clerk.

"Sheet music?"

"No. Piano tuning."

She looks at me blankly a moment: I get the feeling this is not a common request.

"Let me look that up," she finally says.

She taps around on her computer and then takes a map of their megastore and marks off a tiny sliver of it with an orange highlighter.

"There it is." She caps her pen. "You can take the map."

I do, and at first I get lost anyway because it's Powell's and that's what always happens there. But eventually I find their shelf of piano books—the first I pick up is a tatty copy of *Care and Restoration of the Piano*. All the tuning books look as though they were first published during the Harding administration; but then I suppose it's an old profession, and maybe things haven't changed all that much. The curious thing is that back when these books were written, a great many tuners were disabled; schools for the blind would train them in tuning, on the theory that their blindness made them more acutely aware of sound. Later, by the mid–twentieth century, autists were also being trained as tuners—their perfect sense of pitch and their fascination with intricate mechanisms make them ideal for the job.

I set aside the tuning books. There are also some big coffee table books here—one is simply called *The Piano*, with giant foldout diagrams, while others are glossy slabs like *A Hundred Years of Steinway*. I pile them all up and leaf through them. Hmm. Maybe I should get a yard sale piano—a beat-up old Steck or something, just to rip the panels off and leave its workings exposed in a corner of Morgan's room, so he can mess with the mechanisms and—nah, it's still too soon. I pick a coffee table book on piano construction instead. But I have the feeling I might have to come back for the other books eventually. And why not? Focus is a weakness and a strength: you might as well make the strengths as strong as you can.

These fixations don't always work out. One of the strangest news stories in New York over the years has been the legendary subterranean exploits of Darius McCollum. McCollum was first arrested in 1981, at the age of thirteen, for impersonating a subway conductor. Growing up by the 179th Street train yards in Queens, he had memorized the entire New York City subway system by the time he was eight and kept endless notes on the movements of the trains. He hung around the repair yards to learn signaling, electrical repair, and conducting from old train men. They were glad just for the company and gave him uniforms, keys to the system, his own orange emergency lantern—truly everything he ever wanted. The crews loved him and treated him as one of their own.

Only he's not. His record for imposture, for wanting to be a transit employee, keeps him from ever *being* a transit employee—his attempts to apply for the jobs go nowhere. But he's convincing to crewmen who don't know that he isn't one of them and so lovable in his enthusiasm to those who do know that sometimes he drops in to work with them. At other times they'll actually call him in for assistance. For every time McCollum has been nabbed driving a train, there are dozens more that he hasn't been caught. But after spending a few weeks working shifts driving de-icer vehicles, checking for busted electrical equipment, and pulling late night assignments making track inspections, he generally winds up being caught by some administrator. McCollum has been arrested nineteen times now; his most recent capture got him thrown into a maximum security prison for a five-year term as a repeat offender.

He is now confined to his cell twenty-one hours a day—because he is in his own world and nonviolent, he is kept away from the other prisoners for his own safety—and in that cell he glumly hangs up handmade signs on the bars reading TRAIN OUT OF SERVICE. He just wants to be with the trains: it's all he's ever wanted. He could probably be the best crewman NYC's Metropolitan Transportation Authority has ever had. But they say they have no choice.

Yet sometimes—*sometimes*—it can all go right. There's one couple in Los Angeles with a son obsessed by all things relating to trash and recycling. He has memorized the garbage collection routes, the makes and types of disposal vehicles, and he talks of little else. So they arranged with the local garbagemen to have a seventh birthday party for him out at the local landfill. The *Los Angeles Times* sent a reporter to cover it, blissfully unaware that perhaps this boy was—well, even more different than he seemed. "We don't know where this interest in trash came from," they quoted the boy's mother. "He's been this way since he was 2." But both parents say they are fine with him spending his life working with trash, if that's what makes him happy.

"He said he wants to go to college so he can learn to drive a trash truck," the *Times* reporter duly noted.

Morgan is walking between Jennifer and me, holding his schoolbag the way we showed him, and counting steps. "Thirty-one, thirty-two, thirty-three . . ."

Morgan starts skipping, holding on to our hands as though they're bungee cords, bouncing up and then swinging down.

"Morgan," I tell him, "we're going to your new class. Look!"

"Look," he says.

As we walk in, Morgan lets go of us and his schoolbag and runs into the crowded room, immediately descending upon a bucket full of blocks.

"Hi!" A teacher shakes our hands. "You must be . . ."

We must be parents. There are half a dozen kids in the class, and most of their parents are here, too: it's the first day of autism class, an open house with parents and children and teaching specialists milling around. Or rather, the parents and teaching assistants are milling around the perimeter of the classroom, talking; the children are exploring the chairs and tables and toys quietly or while repeating phrases to themselves and flapping their hands with excitement. They play with cars, with blocks, with crayons and jack-in-the-boxes, and— it is the damnedest thing I have ever seen—*they are all playing in parallel.* They are watching what the others are doing, and imitating, but all the while leaving one another alone. It's like watching the pieces of a fabulously strange contrivance, scattered and separated for years, all click suddenly together to form an mysterious whole.

"Are you seeing this?"

Jennifer nods.

"It's like a family reunion."

A father standing by us hears this and laughs.

"Your first time here?" he says.

"Yeah . . . I'm Paul." I shake his hand. "That's Morgan, over there. We've been waiting to get in, but he only just turned the minimum age."

"Three and a half?"

"Mmm-hmm," I nod. "Is your son in this class?"

"That's him over there." He points. "Jamal. In the conductor's hat."

It's true: he's got on overalls and the striped cap, like your classic Casey Jones.

"Likes trains, then?"

"Yes," the father replies dryly. "You could say that."

We watch Morgan move from table to table, circulating and somehow acknowledging the other boys without conversing or doing anything with them. And they are happy to do the same in return. There is no awkwardness at all among them: they are equals. It is as if we have brought a seal to the ocean and watched him shuffle awkwardly off the land to glide effortlessly through the waves, finally within the world he was made for all along.

But surely you cannot just leave them out there like that . . . can you?

When Morgan's diagnosis first came in, all I could think of was: How do I fix him? How do I make him normal again? But there was no again, not really, because there never was a before. He has always been this way: it is who he is. Still, I wanted him to be able to fit in, to not have to feel that he was different. Just some special classes, some special help, I'd figured, and he can get along in the regular school classes, he can be mainstreamed. And I suppose it's a fine thing to fit in, when you can. If he does, that will make things easier. And if he doesn't? . . .

I look around the classroom. Morgan is repeating software dialogue to himself—"Tigger uses a big silver saw"—while Jamal the conductor is lining blocks down a table in a series of straight lines. One boy is lying underneath the table, observing its wooden joinery. Another child has run to the edge of the classroom, where kid-high windows in different geometric shapes open out onto a grassy slope with a flowering tree that lets in little patterns of sunlight; he stares at it, spins around with his eyes closed and hands flapping, and then stops to stare at the tree again.

Where will this lead? I don't know, really. Autists are self-made people: they won't particularly be whatever you are trying to make them into. One writer I know has an autistic child who, after being mainstreamed into a "normal" classroom, was existentially miserable. Everyone knew he was Not One of Them. They picked on him, tormented him, shunned him; at her wits' end, she transferred him into a school for autistic kids. And now, for the first time, he has friends. They e-mail one another, talk on the phone for hours, play geeky computer games together, and they are *happy*. So was their schooling a failure? Do they even fit into any normal schema of success or failure?

Autists are the ultimate square pegs, and the problem with pounding a square peg into a round hole is not that the hammering is hard work. It's that you are destroying the peg. What if normal school makes you abnormally miserable? And what if growing up into normal society makes you a miserable adult? Is that success? Is *that* normal? Do you want to be in the mainstream if it's going to drown you?

"Do you need anything from the supermarket?" I gather up my backpack and open the front door. "I'm heading over there."

My voice sounds big and echoey in the house; it's Friday, the one day Morgan's class doesn't meet, and we have the place to ourselves for the afternoon while Marc takes Morgan out.

"One hundred forty-two," Jennifer mutters from the kitchen. She is counting points while she washes the dishes. Then, louder: "I already went this morning."

"Ah."

I drop my bag and lean into the kitchen to kiss her, which probably screws up her point count, but oh well, and then I head out of the house.

"Milk!" Jennifer yells as I close the front door.

When I get to the market it's full of daytime people like me—at-home parents, freelancers, retirees, students—people who will actually stand around and examine sell-by dates and price per ounce. I'm busy reaching way into the back of the dairy case where the newest milk is hidden, and then I hear it:

"I am not your broom! I am not your broom!"

I peek around at the store's toy aisle and see Morgan belting out a children's song into Marc's ear.

"I didn't know you guys were coming to the store, too."

"Oh, hey! Yeah, we—"

"No longer must I sweep for you for I am not your broom!"

"Hey, little guy." I kneel down next to him. "Are you singing for Uncle Marc?"

He doesn't answer, doesn't look at me, but starts loudly humming the tune instead.

"Morgan, look!" Marc prompts him. "It's Daddy! Say, 'Hi, Daddy!'"

Marc works his hand through a waving motion.

"Now you try it. Go on . . ."

We wait a moment. Nothing, he just keeps humming.

"Well—"

"Hi!" he suddenly yells, and waves glancingly at me.

"Good job, Morgan!"

When Morgan waves, it's with his knuckles facing out and his palm in. Because he sees his palm as he's waving, he thinks that's how I see it. It makes sense, in a way.

"Morgan," Marc says, "are you going to sing for Daddy, too?"

Morgan goes back to humming and inspects a deck of cards on sale.

"Ah well. I need to finish shopping anyway. I'll see you guys back at the house." I lean down and give Morgan a little hug as I leave. He doesn't stop examining his cards. But that's how it is. I come and he sort of notices; I go and he sort of doesn't.

I walk around the market, trying to remember what exactly I came for—milk, bread, razors, and at least one other thing I probably won't recall until I've walked halfway home. I stop in front of the pharmacy section, racking my memory. There are pregnancy kits and baby formula down this aisle; down another are the nasty little cans of Ensure, and denture glue, and all that other mentholated epsom salted arthritic stuff that you have to use when you're old. A father rolls past me with a toddler lolling in his shopping cart; she is trying to balance a bell pepper on her nose. A daughter.

Another child? . . . Do we? . . .

I look up and down the baby aisle, wondering. Pacifiers, formula, little medicine droppers and bibs with teddies on them.

Maybe they'll grow up to be close. Maybe not: they will be their own selves. But life is so long, and every outcome up to the last so uncertain—and when it comes to your child, your confidence cannot extend far past your front door. Not when you are talking about decades, not even when you are talking about days. You cannot trust the state: you cannot trust your friends: you cannot trust the goodness of humanity, which great though it can be is terribly spotty in its delivery. Spouses can divorce, friends can drift, parents die a generation before you—siblings are the only people bound together for an entire lifetime. They are the only remotely sure thing.

Batteries—yes, batteries are the other thing I needed. I grab a couple of chunky D cells off the rickety display near the checkout and pop them up and down in my palm, listening to the distant sound across the market of someone's kid throwing a fit, which is pretty much what you always hear in supermarkets. Only . . .

I look up. Marc is struggling to carry Morgan across the store, looking for me, and Morgan is screaming and flailing in a tangle of limbs, heaving upside down and sideways, and hitting out in every direction while the other shoppers look on.

"Mor—" Marc starts, and nearly gets booted across the face.

"I'm here!" I yell, and run toward them. "What hap—"

"He noticed you were gone, and . . ." I get socked in the chin; my son is thrashing blindly.

"Daddy!" He pummels his hands against me. *"Daddy!"*

"He usually doesn't notice when you leave," Marc says. "I didn't know—"

"Daddy!"

"It's okay . . ."

I hold Morgan and stroke his hair while he sobs.

"You are such a good boy." I sway him back and forth. "You used your words."

"Daddy . . ."

"It's okay," I tell him. "It's okay. I'm right here."

I keep holding him and don't look up for a long time: when I do, the other shoppers are looking at us funny.

"You okay?" I ask Morgan.

He holds me tighter and wipes his nose on my shirt.

The other shoppers stop staring and turn away, though one woman still watches us while she bags her tomatoes. I guess I'm getting used to the stares. So is Jennifer, I think. And Morgan, well . . . he couldn't care less. If we don't make sense to them, that's fine, because we all make sense to each other. And anyway, it's not what they think. It's not a tragedy, it's not a sad story, it's not the movie of the week. It's my family.

FURTHER READING

There are now innumerable works on autism—some quite good, many that are at least well-intentioned, and some that are simply harebrained. But for those just beginning to learn about autism, I think these few books should be your first places to start.

For Parents and Relatives

Between these books you'll get autism from every household angle: from parents, siblings, and autists themselves. And while there are many excellent guides to autism, Baron-Cohen's remains the best way to understand, in one sitting, just what it's all about.

• Andron, Linda, ed. *Our Journey Through High Functioning Autism and Asperger Syndrome: A Roadmap* (2001). For anyone with a newly diagnosed child, reading this book is like walking into a roomful of parents who immediately understand you. These are essays by parents of autistic children, anecdotally describing their child-raising experiences and approaches. In an interesting twist, this volume also includes responses by these children—most are now teenagers or adults—that compare and contrast their own recollection of events.

• Baron-Cohen, Simon, and Patrick Bolton. *Autism: The Facts* (1993). Though a bit creaky now, this brief primer remains one of the handiest introductions to the basics of autism. If you need a hundred-page crash course, this is still the book to go to.

● Grandin, Temple. *Thinking in Pictures* (1996). Grandin's memoir of what it's like to be autistic is a landmark work, and justly so. For many parents of autistic children, this is probably the first book they give to friends and family—even when people cannot grasp neurological theories, they immediately understand a first-person account.

● Karasik, Paul and Judy. *The Ride Together: A Brother and Sister's Memoir of Autism in the Family* (2003). An excellent graphic-narrative memoir—Paul is a cartoonist for *The New Yorker*—by the Karasiks of their autistic brother, David.

Clinical / Theoretical Works

There is a vast and rapidly growing body of medical writings on autism. Uta Frith and Simon Baron-Cohen, though, remain the key figures in theories of autism and in the cutting edge of autism research, and their works provide a crucial grounding to anyone wanting to understand the clinical literature of autism.

● For a wonderful informal account by a neurologist, also see Oliver Sacks's portrayal of Temple Grandin; it is the title essay in his book *An Anthropologist on Mars* (1995).

● Baron-Cohen, Simon, et al., eds. *Understanding Other Minds: Perspectives from Developmental Cognitive Neuroscience* (2nd ed., 2000). A compilation of the most important and provocative medical papers in autism studies; this collection is the standard work in the field and cited in nearly every study on autism. The prose is academic, and the book is priced accordingly. But if you are undertaking a serious study of the current work in autism, you simply have to tackle this book first.

- Baron-Cohen, Simon. *Mindblindness* (1997). A brief but influential expansion by Baron-Cohen upon his earlier work on the autistic "theory of mind."

- Frith, Uta, ed. *Autism and Asperger Syndrome* (1991). As the first work to translate Hans Asperger's pioneering thesis, Frith's book had a major impact on the English-speaking world's understanding of autism. The other essays in the book—covering Leo Kanner's work and studies following autistic children as they develop into adulthood—remain timely as ever. For anyone wanting to understand the modern history of autism, this book is essential.

- Frith, Uta. *Autism: Explaining the Enigma* (2nd ed., 2003). A clearly written treatise synthesizing an array of academic sources. Frith's notion of "weak central coherence"—a literal disintegration of the autistic mind—is generally paired with Baron-Cohen's "theory of mind" as the two most prominent theories explaining autism.

SOURCES

Chapters 1–4

No book-length history has ever been written of the extraordinary history of Peter the Wild Boy. But there is, oddly enough, a forgotten novel written about him: *Peter the Wild Boy*, by C. M. Tennant (1938). It's illustrated with beautiful engravings and is fairly difficult to find.

There is also a fascinating account of another apparent 18th-century case of autism, *Autism in History* by Rab Houston and Uta Frith, which focuses on a Scottish court fight over a landowner whose marriage was annulled due to a ruling of mental incapacity.

An Account of a Savage Girl, Caught Wild in the Woods of Champagne. Edinburgh: A. Kincaid and J. Bell, 1768.

An Enquiry into How the Wild Youth, Lately Taken in the Woods Near Hanover and Now Brought over to England, Could Be Left There. London: H. Parker, 1726.

A New Guide to London: or, Directions to Strangers. London: J. Smith, 1726.

Arbuthnot, John. *The Life and Works of John Arbuthnot.* Edited by George Aitken. Oxford: Clarendon Press, 1892.

"Axtell of Berkhampstead." *Notes and Queries* (December 4, 1869): 478.

Beattie, Lester. *John Arbuthnot: Mathematician and Satirist.* Cambridge: Harvard University Press, 1935.

Bondeson, Jan. *The Feejee Mermaid, and Other Essays in Natural and Unnatural History.* Ithaca: Cornell University Press, 1999.

Boswell, James. *Boswell's Life of Johnson: Together with Boswell's Journal of a*

Tour to the Hebrides and Johnson's Diary of a Journey into North Wales. Edited by George Hill and L. F. Powell. Oxford: Clarendon Press, 1950.

Blumenbach, Johann. *The Anthropological Treatises of Johann Freidreich Blumenbach.* Translated by Thomas Bendyshe. London: Longman, 1865.

Buffon, Georges Louis Leclerc. *Natural History, General and Particular.* London: T. Cadell and M. Davis, 1791.

Clodd, Edward. "Dr. Johnson and Lord Monboddo." In *Johnson Club Papers, by Various Hands,* 31–54. London: Fisher Unwin, 1921.

Cloyd, Emily L. *James Burnett, Lord Monboddo.* Oxford: Clarendon Press, 1972.

Coleman, Everard. "Tailed Africans." *Notes and Queries* (December 1, 1888): 433.

Cotton, Evan. "A Calcutta Painter." *Bengal Past and Present* (1927): 116–119. (Article on John Alefounder, portraitist of Peter the Wild Boy.)

De Saussure, Cesar. *A Foreign View of England in 1725–29: The Letters of Monsieur Cesar de Saussure to His Family.* London: Caliban Books, 1995.

Defoe, Daniel. *Mere Nature Delineated—or, A Body Without a Soul.* London: T. Warner, 1726.

The Devil to Pay at St. James's. London: A. Moore, 1727.

"Events of October 27." *Gentleman's Magazine* 21 (November 1751): 522. (An account of a jail fire in Norwich involving Peter the Wild Boy.)

Fairholt, Frederick. *Eccentric and Remarkable Characters.* London: Bentley's Cabinet Library, 1848.

Graham, Henry Grey. *Scottish Men of Letters of the Eighteenth Century.* London: Adam and Charles Black, 1901.

Gray, W. Forbes. "A Forerunner of Darwin." *Fortnightly Review* (1929): 112–122.

Hackwood, R. W. "Burial Place of George I." *Notes and Queries* (July 21, 1888): 51.

Hatton, Ragnhild. *George I, Elector and King.* Cambridge: Harvard University Press, 1978.

Houston, Rab, and Uta Frith. *Autism in History: The Case of Hugh Blair of Borgue.* Oxford: Blackwell Publishers, 2000.

Hutton, Laurence. "The Literary Landmarks of Edinburgh." *Harper's New Monthly Magazine.* (March 1891): 609–635.

Jones, Arthur, ed. *Hertfordshire 1731–1800, as Recorded in the Gentleman's Magazine.* Hertfordshire Publications, 1993.

London Journal January 20, 1727–1728. (Article on visit by Peter the Wild Boy to the vicar of Hemelhemsted.)

"Lord Monboddo, His Ancestors and His Heirs." *The Month* (1871): 440–464.

Lovejoy, Arthur. "Monboddo and Rousseau." In *Essays on the History of Ideas,* 38–61. Baltimore: Johns Hopkins University Press, 1960.

SOURCES

Knight, William Angus. *Lord Monboddo and Some of His Contemporaries*. London: J. Murray, 1900.

MacDiarmid, Hugh. *Scottish Eccentrics*. London: Routledge, 1936.

Maclean, Charles. *The Wolf Children*. London: Allen Lane, 1977.

The Manifesto of Lord Peter. London: J. Roberts, 1726.

McCowan, Theodore, and Kenneth Kennedy, eds. *Climbing Man's Family Tree: A Collection of Major Writings on Human Phylogeny, 1699 to 1971*. Englewood Cliffs, N.J.: Prentice-Hall, 1971.

Monboddo, Lord (James Burnett). *Antient Metaphysics: or, The Science of Universals*. Edinburgh: J. Balfour and Company, 1779.

The Most Wonderful Wonder That Ever Appear'd to the Wonder of the British Nation. London: A. More, 1726.

Mundy, P. D., and A. R. Bayley. "Peter the Wild Boy." *Notes and Queries* (February 21, 1914): 146; (March 14, 1914): 211.

New, Anthony. "Hertfordshire Churches." *Hertfordshire Countryside* (1963): 346–347.

Newton, Michael. *Savage Girls and Wild Boys: A History of Feral Children*. London: Faber & Faber, 2002.

Novak, Maximillian. *Defoe and the Nature of Man*. Oxford: Oxford University Press, 1963.

Obituary of Peter the Wild Boy. *Gentleman's Magazine* 57 (March 1785): 236.

Owen, J. P. "Lord Monboddo and the Darwinian Theory." *Notes and Queries* (June 22, 1895): 486.

Page, William. *The Victoria History of the Country of Hertford*. London: University of London, 1971 (3 vols., 1902–1914).

"Peter the Wild Boy." *Notes and Queries* (September 27, 1884): 248; (October 11, 1884): 293–294; (November 15, 1884): 395; (December 20, 1884): 593.

Pevsner, Nikolaus. *Hertfordshire*. London: Penguin Books, 1953.

Plunkett, George. *Rambles in Old Norwich*. Lavenham, Suffolk: Terence Dalton, 1990.

Ramsay, John. *Scotland and Scotsmen*. Edinburgh: Blackwood & Sons, 1888.

Schneider, Louis, ed. *The Scottish Moralists on Human Nature and Society*. Chicago: University of Chicago Press, 1967.

Shand, Alexander. "Lord Monboddo and the Old Scottish Judges." *Cornhill Magazine* (April 1901): 482–494.

Slotkin, J. S., ed. *Readings in Early Anthropology*. London: Methuen, 1965.

Shattuck, Roger. *The Forbidden Experiment: The Story of the Wild Boy of Aveyron*. London: Secker & Warburg, 1980.

Stark, Werner. *The Social Bond: An Investigation into the Bases of Law-Abidingness*. New York: Fordham University Press, 1976.

Steensma, Robert C. *Dr. John Arbuthnot*. Boston: Twayne Publishers, 1979.

Swift, Jonathan. *Works of Jonathan Swift*. London: Bickers & Son, 1883.

———— (attributed). *It Cannot Rain but It Pours: or, London Strow'd with Rarities*. London: J. Roberts, 1726.

Tallack, T. R. "Peter the Wild Boy." *Notes and Queries* (October 24, 1885): 335.

Walker, John. *The Wild Boy of Bohemia; or, The Force of Nature. A Melodrama, in Two Acts*. NY: Samuel French, 1879.

Weekly Journal, or British Gazeteer, January 22, 1726. (Item on Peter.)

————, June 3, 1727.

Wokler, Robert. "Apes and Races in the Scottish Enlightenment: Monboddo and Kames on the Nature of Man." In *Philosophy and Science in the Scottish Enlightnement*, edited by Peter Jones, 145–168. Edinburgh: John Donald Publishers Ltd., 1988.

Chapter 5

Asperger's and Kanner's papers remain key documents to understanding autism's past and present. I cannot recommend Bettelheim's work for anything other than historical reasons; Pollak's devastating exposé, on the other hand, should be widely read for its cautionary portrayal of how psychoanalysis's disdain for basic protocols of evidence and testing allowed it to become a breeding ground for charlatans.

Though not mentioned in this chapter, Oliver Sacks's *The Man Who Mistook His Wife for a Hat* contains a very interesting account of the deleterious effect of another type of broken-up family—his essay "The Twins" describes the effects of the separation of a pair of twin autistic brothers.

Asperger, Hans. " 'Autistic Psychopathy' in Childhood." In *Autism and Asperger Syndrome*, edited by Uta Frith, 37–92 (1944; translation 1991).

————."Problems of Infantile Autism." *Communication* (1979): 45–52.

Bettelheim, Bruno. *The Empty Fortress: Infantile Autism and the Birth of the Self*. New York: Macmillan, 1967.

Frith, Uta, ed. *Autism and Asperger Syndrome*. Cambridge: Cambridge University Press, 1991.

Frith, Uta. "Asperger and His Syndrome." In *Autism and Asperger Syndrome*, 1–36.

Kanner, Leo. "Autistic Disturbances of Affective Contact." *Nervous Child* (1943): 217–250.

————. "Follow-Up Study of Eleven Autistic Children Originally Reported in 1943." *Journal of Autism and Childhood Schizophrenia* (1971): 119–145.

————, et al. "How Far Can Autistic Children Go in Matters of Social Adaptation?" *Journal of Autism and Childhood Schizophrenia* (1972): 9–33.

Pollak, Richard. *The Creation of Dr. B: A Biography of Bruno Bettelheim*. New York: Simon & Schuster, 1997.

Sacks, Oliver. *The Man Who Mistook His Wife for a Hat: And Other Clinical Tales*. New York: Harper & Row, 1987.

Wing, Lorna. "The Relationship Between Asperger's Syndrome and Kanner's Autism." In *Autism and Asperger Syndrome*, edited by Uta Frith, 93–121.

Chapter 7

An entertaining account of John Fransham can be found in the *Dictionary of National Biography*, in addition to Saint's biography. (Saint is very hard to find, but UC Berkeley has a copy.)

Asperger, Hans. "'Autistic Psychopathy' in Childhood." In *Autism and Asperger Syndrome*, edited by Uta Frith, 37–92 (1944; translation 1991).

Baron-Cohen, Simon, et al. *Understanding Other Minds: Perspectives from Developmental Cognitive Neuroscience*. 2nd ed. Oxford: Oxford University Press, 2000.

————. "Does Autism Cluster Geographically? A Research Note." *Autism* 3, no. 1 (1999): 39–43.

————. "Is There a Link Between Engineering and Autism?" *Autism* 1, no. 1 (1997): 101–109.

————. "Does Autism Occur More Often in Families of Physicists, Engineers, and Mathematicians?" *Autism* 2, no. 3 (1998): 296–301.

————. "A Mathematician, a Physicist and a Computer Scientist with Asperger Syndrome: Performance on Folk Psychology and Folk Physics Tests." *Neurocase* 5, no. 6 (1999): 475–483.

Baron-Cohen, Simon. "Theory of Mind and Autism: A Fifteen-Year Review." In Simon Baron-Cohen et al., *Understanding Other Minds*, 3–20.

————. "Autism: Deficits in Folk Psychology Exist Alongside Superiority in Folk Physics." In Simon Baron-Cohen et al., *Understanding Other Minds*, 73–82.

Bell, E. T. *Men of Mathematics*. London: Victor Gollancz, 1937.

Frith, Uta, ed. *Autism and Asperger Syndrome*. Cambridge: Cambridge University Press, 1991.

Frith, Uta. "Asperger and His Syndrome." In *Autism and Asperger Syndrome*, 1–36.

Gillberg, Christopher. "Clinical and Neurobiological Aspects of Asperger Syndrome in Six Family Studies." In *Autism and Asperger Syndrome*, edited by Uta Frith, 122–146.

MacFarlane, Alexander. *Lectures on Ten British Mathematicians of the Nineteenth Century*. New York: John Wiley & Sons, 1916.

Pollak, Richard. *The Creation of Dr. B: A Biography of Bruno Bettelheim*. New York: Simon & Schuster, 1997.

Saint, W. *Memoirs of the Life, Character, Opinions, and Writings of That Learned and Eccentric Man, the Late John Fransham of Norwich*. Norwich: C. Berryt, 1811.

Tager-Flusberg, Helen. "Language and Understanding Mind: Conections in Autism." In Simon Baron-Cohen et al., *Understanding Other Minds*, 124–149.

Wheelwright, Sally, and Simon Baron-Cohen. "The Link Between Autism and Such Skills as Engineering, Maths, Physics, and Computing." *Autism: The International Journal of Research and Practice* 5, no. 2 (2001): 223–227.

Wing, Lorna. "The Relationship Between Asperger's Syndrome and Kanner's Autism." In *Autism and Asperger Syndrome*, edited by Uta Frith, 93–121.

Chapter 8

The University of Washington Autism Center, as well as the associated efforts nearby at Microsoft, will probably have progressed into all sorts of new work by the time this book reaches the shelves. Fittingly enough, online sources are probably the best place to go for news of their current projects.

Herken, Rolf, ed. *The Universal Turing Machine*. New York: Oxford University Press, 1988.

Hodges, Andrew. *Alan Turing: The Enigma*. 2nd ed. London: Vintage, 1992.

Linn, Allison. "Microsoft, UW Develop Program to Treat Autism Syndrome Online." *Seattle Times*, March 11, 2002.

Rivlin, Gary. *The Plot to Get Bill Gates*. New York: Times Books, 1999.

Chapter 10

Synaesthesia

Cytowic, Baron-Cohen, and Harrison are the modern authorities in the field. Not mentioned in my chapter, but worth seeking out, is a very curious series of letters in *Notes and Queries* (5th series, January–June 1874) under the title "Realising the Signs of Thought." They discuss the seemingly inexplicable mental associations that readers held between numbers, vectors, and geometric figures.

Bacon, Francis. *Sylva*. 6th ed. London: Rawley, 1651.

Baron-Cohen, Simon, and John E. Harrison, eds. *Synaesthesia: Classic and Contemporary Readings*. Oxford: Blackwell Publishers, 1997.

Baron-Cohen, Simon, et al. *Understanding Other Minds: Perspectives from Developmental Cognitive Neuroscience*. 2nd ed. New York: Oxford University Press, 2000.

Castel, Louis Bertrand. *Explanation of the Ocular Harpsichord, upon Shew to the Public*. London: S. Hooper & Co., 1757.

Corcoran, Rhiannon. "Theory of Mind in Other Clinical Conditions: Is a Selective 'Theory of Mind' Deficit Exclusive to Autism?" In Simon Baron-Cohen et al., *Understanding Other Minds*, 391–421.

Critchley, Edmund. "Synaestheia: Possible Mechanisms." In *Synaesthesia*, edited by Simon Baron-Cohen and John E. Harrison, 259–268.

Cytowic, Richard E. *Synaesthesia: A Union of the Senses*. New York: Springer-Verlag, 1989.

————. "Synaesthesia: Phenomenology and Neuropsychology: A Review of Current Knowledge." In *Synaesthesia*, edited by Simon Baron-Cohen and John E. Harrison, 17–39.

Field, George. *Chromatics: or, Essay on the Analogy and Harmony of Colours*. London: Newman, 1817.

————. *Outlines of Analogical Philosophy, Being a Primary View of the Principles, Relations, and Purposes of Nature, Science, and Art*. London: 1839.

————. *Tritogenea: or, A Brief Outline of the Universal System*. 3rd ed. London: 1846.

Frith, Christopher, and Eraldo Paulesu. "The Physiological Basis of Synaesthesia." In *Synaesthesia*, edited by Simon Baron-Cohen and John E. Harrison, 123–147.

Galton, Francis. *Inquiries into the Human Faculty*. London: Dent, 1883.

Gray, Jeffrey, et al. "Possible Implications of Synaesthesia for the Hard Question of Conciousness." In *Synaesthesia*, edited by Simon Baron-Cohen and John E. Harrison, 173–181.

Happe, Francesca. "Parts and Wholes, Meaning and Minds: Central Coherence and Its Relation to Theory of Mind." In Simon Baron-Cohen et al., *Understanding Other Minds*, 203–221.

Kraus, Joseph. "The Smell Organ." *Science and Invention* (June 1922): 21–22.

Luria, A. R. *The Mind of a Mnemonist*. New York: Basic Books, 1968.

"Music as Colour: Screen Accompaniment to Compositions." *The Times* (London), March 20, 1914: 11.

"Perfumes and Perfumery." *Scientific American* (July 25, 1863): 52–53. (Contains an account of Piesse & Lubin's operations.)

Piesse, Charles Henry. *Olfactics and the Physical Senses*. London: Piesse & Lubin, 1887.

Piesse, G. W. Septimus. *Chymical, Natural, and Physical Magic*. London: Longman, 1865.

————. *The Art of Perfumery, and the Methods of Obtaining the Odors of Plants*. 2nd U.S. ed. Philadelphia: Lindsay & Blakiston, 1867.

————. "The London Exhibition—Perfumery." *Scientific American* (December 6, 1862): 357–358.

———— Obituary. *Journal of the Chemical Society* (1883): 255.

————, et al. "Analogy Between Colours and Musical Sounds." *Notes and Queries* (June 21, 1862): 485; (July 12, 1862): 36; (July 26, 1862): 79–80.

Rimington, A. M. *Colour-Music: The Art of Mobile Colour*. London: Hutchinson, 1911.

Rimmel, Eugene. *The Book of Perfumes*. 2nd ed. London: Chapman and Hall, 1865.

Sagarin, Edward. *The Science and Art of Perfumery*. New York: McGraw-Hill, 1945.

Van Campen, Cretien. "Artistic and Psychological Experiments with Synaesthesia." *Leonardo* 32, no. 1 (1999): 9–14.

James Henry Pullen

No book-length work has been published on Pullen, but his story is well contextualized in Donald Treffert's history of savantism, and both Ward and Wright give thorough histories of Earlswood Asylum.

Down, John Langdon. *On Some Mental Affectations of Childhood and Youth.* London: J & A Churchill, 1887.

Goddard, Henry Herbert. *Feeble-Mindedness: Its Causes and Consequences.* New York: Macmillan, 1914.

Ireland, William Witherspoon. *The Mental Affections of Children, Idiocy, Imbecility, and Insanity.* London: J & A Churchill, 1898.

Sano, Frederick. "James Henry Pullen, the Genius of Earlswood." *Journal of Mental Science* (July 1918): 251–267.

Seguin, Edouard. *Idiocy: Its Treatment and the Psychological Method.* New York: W. Wood, 1866.

Tredgold, A. F. *Mental Deficiency (Amentia).* 4th ed. New York: William Wood & Co., 1922.

Treffert, Donald. *Extraordinary People.* New York: Harper & Row, 1988.

Ward, O. Conor. *John Langdon Down: A Caring Pioneer.* London: Royal Society of Medicine Press, 1998.

Wright, David. *Mental Disability in Victorian England: The Earlswood Asylum, 1847–1901.* Oxford: Oxford University Press, 2001.

Wynter, Andrew. *Our Social Bees.* London: Robert Hardwicke, 1861.

—————. *The Borderlands of Insanity.* New York: G. P. Putnam's Sons, 1875.

Chapter 12

In addition to the books and articles listed below, the Mind Reading software containing "The Library of Human Emotions" can be found at www.human-emotions.com.

Colby, K. M., and D. C. Smith. "Computers in the Treatment of Nonspeaking Autistic Children." *Current Psychiatric Therapies* 11, no. 1 (1971): 1–17.

Darwin, Charles. *The Expression of the Emotions in Man and Animals.* London: John Murray, 1872.

Dautenhahn, Kerstin, and A. Billard. "Games Children with Autism Can Play with Robota, a Humanoid Robotic Doll." In *Universal Access and Assistive Technology*, 179–190. London: Springer-Verlag, 2002.

Dautenhahn, Kerstin, et al. "Robotic Playmates: Analyzing Interactive Competencies of Children with Autism Playing with a Mobile Robot." In *Socially Intelligent Agents: Creating Relationships with Computers and Robots*, 117–124. Norwell: Klumer Academic Publishers, 2002.

Dautenhahn, Kerstin, and Iain Werry. "A Quantitative Technique for

Analyzing Robot-Human Interactions." *Proceedings of the 2002 IEEE/ RSJ International Conference on Intelligent Robots and Systems*, 1132–1138. Lausanne, Switzerland: IEEE/RSJ, 2002.

De Boulogne, G. B. Duchenne. *The Mechanism of Human Facial Expression*. Cambridge: Cambridge University Press, 1990 (reprint of 1862 ed.).

Grenville, Bruce, ed. *The Uncanny: Experiments in Cyborg Culture*. Vancouver: Arsenal Pulp Press, 2002.

Raine, Craig. *A Martian Sends a Postcard Home*. New York: Oxford University Press, 1979.

Sainsbury, Claire. *Martian in the Playground: Understanding the Schoolchild with Asperger's Syndrome*. Bristol, Eng.: Lucky Duck Publishing, 2000.

Werry, Iain, et al. "Can Social Interaction Skills Be Taught by a Social Agent? The Role of a Robotic Mediator in Autism Therapy." 2001. At www.aurora-project.com.

Wood, Gaby. *Edison's Eve: A Magical History of the Quest for Mechanical Life*. New York: Knopf, 2002.

Chapter 13

Thanks to Michiel Odijk for his assistance on the mathematical nature of timetables. He certainly knows the subject—his doctoral dissertation at the University of Delft was titled *Railway Timetable Generation*, and he creates schedules for Dutch Railways. There are numerous online sites for timetable collectors, and their ranks are growing constantly; the Australian Association of Timetable Collectors *Table Talk* article mentioned can be found at www.aattc. org.au/times298.htm.

Bernhard, Thomas. *Concrete*. Translated by David McLintock. Chicago: University of Chicago Press, 1986.

Gould, Stephen Jay. "Five Weeks." In *Questioning the Millennium*, 163–179. New York: Harmony Books, 1997.

Schawlow, Arthur R. *Optics and Laser Spectroscopy, Bell Telephone Laboratories, 1951–1961, and Stanford University Since 1961*. Regional Oral History Office, University of California, Berkeley, 1996. (The Schawlow interview can also be found at the University of California's online archive at ark.cdlib.org.)

Chapter 14

The Liberty Dog Program depends on the kindness of others—no state money is used, and they always have far more requests than dogs or trainers to fulfill them. So donations are very welcome: you can find them at libertydogprogram.com.

Chevigny, Hector. *My Eyes Have a Cold Nose*. New Haven: Yale University Press, 1946.
Grandin, Temple. *Thinking in Pictures: And Other Reports from My Life with Autism*. New York: Vintage Books, 1996.
Sacks, Oliver. *An Anthropologist on Mars: Seven Paradoxical Tales*. New York: Knopf, 1995.

Chapter 15

Hippolyte Taine's still very readable and worthwhile article "Lingual Development in Babyhood" is on pages 129–137 of the June 1876 issue of *Popular Science Monthly*.

Taine, Hippolyte. *On Intelligence*. London: L. Reeve & Co., 1871.

Chapter 16

Darger's work is archived and displayed at the American Museum of Folk Art in Manhattan, but there is also work afoot to re-create his room in Chicago; all its contents were carefully saved after his death. The essential published source is MacGregor's book, a lavish and weighty volume that sets a new standard in art history and publishing.

Robert FitzRoy's life has been relatively obscure, save for Mellersh's 1968 biography. But as of this writing, a new biography by Peter Nichols is going to press under the title *Evolution's Captain*.

Ades, Dawn. "The Transcendental Surrealism of Joseph Cornell." In Kynaston McShine, *Joseph Cornell*, 15–42.

Cornell, Joseph. *Joseph Cornell's Theater of the Mind: Selected Diaries, Letters, and Files*. Edited by Mary Ann Caws. London: Thames & Hudson, 1994.

Frith, Uta. *Autism: Explaining the Enigma*. Oxford: Blackwell Publishing, 2003.

Hartigan, Lynda. "Joseph Cornell: A Biography." In Kynaston McShine, *Joseph Cornell*, 91–120.

Hayes, Brian. "The Weatherman." *American Scientist* (Jan./Feb. 2001): 10–14.

MacGregor, John. *Henry Darger: In the Realms of the Unreal*. New York: Delano Greenidge Editions LLC, 2002.

McShine, Kynaston, ed. *Joseph Cornell*. New York: Museum of Modern Art, 1990.

Mellersh, H. E. L. *FitzRoy of the Beagle*. London: Hart-Davis, 1968.

Richardson, Lewis Fry. *Weather Prediction by Numerical Process*. Cambridge: Cambridge University Press, 1922.

———. *Collected Papers of Lewis Fry Richardson*. Edited by Oliver Ashford et al. New York: Cambridge University Press, 1993.

Waldman, Diane. *Joseph Cornell: Master of Dreams*. New York: Harry Abrams, 2002.

Wing, Lorna, et al. "Prevalence of Autism and Related Conditions in Adults in a Mental Handicap Hospital." *Applied Research on Mental Retardation* 3 (1982): 303–317.

Chapter 17

A search through *The New York Times* will uncover numerous articles on subway impostor Darius McCollum, but the most insightful account is Jeff Tietz's for *Harper's*, which posits what I think many have suspected all along—that McCollum is a case where an undiagnosed autism spectrum disorder has caught him in the gears of the criminal justice system.

Tietz, Jeff. "The Boy Who Loved Transit: How the System Failed an Obsession." *Harper's* (May 2002).

Thomas, Wendy. "Cakes and Crafts at the Dump." *Los Angeles Times*, December 8, 2002.

Acknowledgments

This book is dedicated, in every sense, to Morgan. You are the best son in the world, ever, anywhere. And my wife, Jennifer, has guided and encouraged this book—as well as its sometimes hapless author—through every day of its existence.

Many thanks to Marc Thomas, for being the best uncle any boy could have.

A belated but much deserved ovation for our pediatrician, Dr. Amy Whalen, for telling us early on what we needed to hear, even when we didn't want to listen.

My great appreciation goes to the parents and instructors who appear in this book, especially Barb Avila and Bruce Thomas; their work with Morgan has meant so much to his growth.

Many professionals in the field generously shared their time and work with me on my travels—including, but certainly not limited to, Reverend Peter Hart, Lili Cheng, Dr. Simon Baron-Cohen, Dr. Fiona Scott, Professor Kirsten Dautenhahn, Sergeant Thom and Barb McGovern, Ricky Jay, and Dr. Maria Asperger. Thanks, too, to Craig Raine for letting me quote from his work.

I am always amazed that books manage to exist at all, given the odds facing their creation, and for beating those odds my many thanks go to my agent, Michelle Tessler, and to editors Colin Dickerman and Charlotte Cole.

ABOUT THE AUTHOR

Paul Collins is the author of *Sixpence House* and *Banvard's Folly*. He edits the Collins Library imprint of McSweeney's Books, and his work has appeared in *New Scientist, The Village Voice,* and *Business 2.0.*

A NOTE ON THE TYPE

This old-style face is named after the Frenchman Robert Granjon, a sixteenth-century letter cutter whose italic types have often been used with the romans of Claude Garamond. The origins of this face, like those of Garamond, lie in the late-fifteenth-century types used by Aldus Manutius in Italy. A good face for setting text in books, magazines, and periodicals.